Life Equity

Life Equity

Realize Your True Value
and Pursue Your Passions
at Any Stage in Life

MARSHA BLACKBURN

THOMAS NELSON
Since 1798

NASHVILLE   DALLAS   MEXICO CITY   RIO DE JANEIRO   BEIJING

Published in Nashville, Tennessee, by Thomas Nelson. Thomas Nelson is a registered trademark of Thomas Nelson, Inc.

Thomas Nelson, Inc., titles may be purchased in bulk for educational, business, fund-raising, or sales promotional use. For information, please e-mail SpecialMarkets@ThomasNelson.com.

Scripture quotations marked NIV are from HOLY BIBLE: NEW INTERNATIONAL VERSION®. © 1973, 1978, 1984 by International Bible Society. Used by permission of Zondervan Publishing House. All rights reserved.

Scripture quotations marked NLT are from *Holy Bible*, New Living Translation. © 1996. Used by permission of Tyndale House Publishers, Inc., Wheaton, Illinois 60189. All rights reserved.

Library of Congress Cataloging-in-Publication Data

Blackburn, Marsha.
  Life equity : realize your true value and pursue your passions at any stage in life / Marsha Blackburn.
    p. cm.
  Includes bibliographical references.
    1. Women—Psychology. 2. Self-esteem in women. 3. Self-perception in women.
  4. Self-acceptance in women. 5. Leadership in women. I. Title.
  HQ1206.B447 2008
  155.6'33—dc22   2008023071

Printed in the United States of America

08 09 10 11 12 QW 6 5 4 3 2 1

IN MEMORY

Ella Jospehine Barber Meeks
Emmie Josephine Meeks Morgan

DEDICATED TO

Mary Josephine Morgan Wedgeworth
Mary Morgan Blackburn Ketchel

Each a woman of influence, intellect and strength

Contents

FOREWORD

I had a conversation this week with my mother, who, at seventy-seven, is having her first experience with a personal trainer. The human body is amazing, isn't it? How it transforms itself with just a little bit of encouragement.

The true being inside the human body, though, is somewhat trickier to uncover but much more magnificent to set free. In *Life Equity*, Marsha Blackburn gives women the tools to do exactly this. It is truly possible, as Marsha shows us, to use the rich talents and experiences we have each been given to pursue our dreams—no matter our age.

At this time in history, more than ever before, it is vital that women understand the crucial roles we play in our civic and philanthropic communities, our churches and schools, and in our world. We're each wired in a unique way, with individual gifts and abilities, and the real world is desperate for the kind of leadership that we are capable of providing, a style of leadership that is built on nurture and encouragement.

Whether we realize it or not, as we live and grow, we accumulate a toolset, which combined with our passion and strengths enables us to move with confidence to the next stage of our lives—lives energized in the pursuit of our particular dreams. Lives filled with meaning.

—Amy Grant
  singer, songwriter

Four Women / Four Questions

Julie opened her leather-bound day planner and began an absentminded doodle on the space for Monday's tasks. There was plenty of doodle room. The day was wide open, as was most of the rest of the week.

Oh, there was lunch with a friend on Tuesday, the women's Bible study she led on Wednesdays, and a Friday-night dinner party for her doctor-husband's partners and their wives. But little else.

In previous years, this same space on the calendar would have been filled with events, tasks, and objectives—every day brimming with responsibility and packed with purpose. But a few weeks ago she had sent her "baby" off to college in another state. Her oldest had flown the nest a year earlier.

Julie had married young and yet managed to simultaneously get her husband through medical school and start a family. She was bright, dynamic, organized, and a proven achiever. What's more, people had always been drawn to her strong personality and confidence. Whether in support of her husband, her children, or her church, everything to which she had put her hand during the last twenty years had succeeded. But now . . . ?

With a sigh Julie looked down at the doodle she'd been tracing over and over with her pen. It was a big question mark.

Barely forty-five years old, she knew the question her soul was posing:

Am I finished?

———————

Jamie leaned back in her Euro-styled "ergonomic" desk chair and scanned the wall of her corner office. A neat grid of framed diplomas, awards, and letters of congratulations offered silent testimony to the talent and drive that had made her at thirty-seven the youngest woman ever to make VP at the Fortune 500 company that had been her personal corporate ladder since business school.

By every outward measure, Jamie had arrived. Could it be that she was really considering walking away from it? Now?

She was indeed. For what only her closest confidants knew was that Jamie was bored. Sure, the prospect of spending the next twenty-five years as a well-paid, stock-optioned, golden-parachuted cog in a giant corporate machine appealed to her need for security. But it sure didn't quicken her pulse. And for Jamie, that was a problem.

For more than a year an idea for a new business venture had been brewing in her. It was a flash of inspiration that seemed to hold the promise of exciting new challenges and tremendous rewards—financial and emotional. But it would mean taking a leap into the unknown.

Lately, whenever she thought about flinging herself into that abyss, an invisible thug named Fear would kick down her door and take a seat on her chest. As if that weren't enough, Fear tended to use that perch on her rib cage to whisper a haunting question in her ear:

What if you fall on your face, Jamie? Now won't that be humiliating?

———————

Not once, in three decades of marriage, family rearing, and community service, had it occurred to Becky—even for a moment—that she would ever find herself in this position.

Alone. Humiliated. Fifty-four. And utterly starting over.

The truly galling part of it all was being so completely blindsided by the dual revelations of John's infidelity and fiscal irresponsibility. *Was I really that blind? Could I possibly be that clueless?*

Now, as her twin embarrassments of bankruptcy and divorce were grinding through the legal system, she found herself on the hunt for both an apartment and a job.

Thirty-three years of homeroom mothering, Cub Scout pack leading, Homeowners' Association administrating, PTA fundraising, and community theater event planning had endued Becky with a powerful set of skills—but with no conventional résumé.

Out of a clear blue sky, a tornado had danced right through the center of Becky's world. Now she stood amid the rubble of her life with a lump in her throat and a question on her lips:

Who will recognize what I have to offer?

———————

Caitlin took a deep, cleansing breath and scrolled through another page of online job listings in the Nonprofit/Humanitarian section. It had been almost four years since she graduated from that prestigious Southern university, and though she had been consistently employed all that time, she still hadn't found her "true calling."

Perhaps her dubious father had been right about the professional utility of a sociology degree. "Does this mean you want to pursue a rewarding career as a *socialist*?" he used to tease. Of course, he knew that her political bent was decidedly conservative.

The impulse that had attracted her to sociology as an area of study was the same one that now kept her from feeling satisfied in any of the "normal" jobs she'd held. She cared deeply about people. She was idealistic and passionate and bright. She wanted her life to count for something.

Caitlin needed to know she was going to leave the world—at least her little piece of it—better than she found it. To all those around her, she was still her characteristically confident self. But inwardly she waged a constant wrestling match with self-doubt.

In her most introspective moments, a single question presented itself over and over, like a slow-blinking warning light on the dashboard of her heart:

Do I have what it takes to make a real difference?

I've Been Down That Road

There are no laurels in life . . . just new challenges.
—KATHARINE HEPBURN

I have given them new names, but the individuals I described on the preceding pages are real. They are amazing, talented ladies. I share their stories because, in one form or another, the questions they have asked are being asked by millions of women in this country. As I travel and meet with women from other countries, I am discovering those questions are, in fact, universal.

I have heard these kinds of fears and uncertainties voiced many times. I have voiced some of them myself.

You see, on January 3, 2003, I stepped through the ornate bronze doors of the Capitol building in Washington DC, headed for the House Chamber, and took my seat in the 108th Congress of the United States. A few months earlier I had become the first Tennessee woman ever elected to Congress in her own right. (Several pioneering Volunteer State women had finished out the terms of their deceased relatives in decades past, but none had initiated her run for this office.)

Along the road that led me to that moment, I had the privilege of talking with thousands of women. I heard their hopes and aspirations, fears and frustrations. And in the exciting years since, I have spoken with thousands more, of all ages and from all walks of life.

In the course of those rich conversations, some common themes have emerged. For one thing, I am deeply impressed by how many women genuinely hunger to do more, be more, and have a bigger impact on their communities and nation. But I have also been struck by how very many of these accomplished, intelligent ladies are hampered by self-doubt and fear.

> Because women are such natural team players and consensus builders, many may simply view a strong desire to lead as, well, a bit rude.

Though they may not think of it this way, what these women aspire to can be encapsulated in a single word—*leadership*.

Leadership is a word much used and often abused. The shelves of our bookstores sag with tomes promising to teach it. Arenas are consistently filled with eager corporate climbers hoping to master its secrets.

For too long and for too many, the word *leadership* has had a masculine ring to it. In fact, I have encountered many amazingly talented and capable women who have trouble identifying with the concept of leadership as a resonant goal for themselves. "I'm just not *that* kind of woman," they say as they compare themselves to the Hollywood stereotype of the hard, humorless, driven climber. In fact, because women are such natural team players and consensus builders, many may simply view a strong desire to lead as, well, a bit rude.

But in every case, if I speak instead of *influence*—if I ask them if they would like to be a more positive influence in their world— they invariably give me an impassioned *"Yes!"* John Maxwell, one of the world's foremost authorities on leadership, has repeatedly pointed out that leadership and influence are synonymous concepts.[1]

Furthermore, if you define leadership as the art of getting a group of people working together effectively toward a common goal—what one prominent corporate consultant calls "getting everyone in the boat rowing in the same direction"[2]—then women bring some mighty powerful leadership skills to the table. And oh, how we need them.

Way back in 1992, *Megatrends* author John Naisbitt recognized an emerging and important approach to leadership at which women excelled. In their book *Megatrends for Women*, Naisbitt and coauthor Patricia Aburdene describe this trend toward a "women's leadership style," which is based on openness, trust, ongoing education, compassion, and understanding.[3]

I note with interest the growing chorus of experts who recognize that this "women's style" of leadership is precisely what is called for in this volatile, uncharted new century. It is a style of leadership that

- empowers individuals instead of making demands,
- restructures organizations instead of controlling from the top down,
- chooses to teach rather than issue orders,

- excels in role modeling in place of decreeing,
- values openness rather than rigid control of information, and
- communicates with a focus on listening as much as or more than on talking.

In a day in which we face unprecedented challenges—locally, nationally, and globally—far too many prospective women leaders are standing in the shallows. They look with half-longing, half-trepidation at the deeper waters.

They long to dive into the challenges and make a difference. But holding them back are questions—questions like the ones posed in the stories of the four women on the preceding pages. I hear other questions too.

"How do I break into, or get around, the good ol' boy network?"

"Where are the mentors who can show me the way?"

"Where do I start?"

It's not about demanding our rights. It's about deploying our gifts.

I write today because we must dive in. It's not about demanding our rights. It's about deploying our gifts. It's not about glass ceilings, quotas, and symbolic progress. It's about successfully shouldering responsibility because we're good at it and we're needed—whether others recognize it or not—and it is vitally important.

Why? Because our nation is being robbed.

We are living at a moment of unprecedented challenges in our nation's history. Some are social. Some are economic. Others are cultural. And in each case, our nation awaits the innovative and difference-making leadership of women.

That is why it is our responsibility to accept a changing role for ourselves as new doors open; to be fluid in moving from one arena to another, always taking with us the skills we have acquired; to welcome new opportunities as they are presented to us; to acknowledge with grace, rather than embarrassment, our accomplishments, successes, and victories; and to serve as guides to others who would follow in our footsteps.

Here is exciting news: there is a key truth that will unlock all of these extraordinary possibilities for you—one that forms the central message of my life and of this book.

That simple but powerful truth is this: your accumulated skills go with you. The ordinary, everyday tasks you have been performing are actually the foundation for getting you where you want to go. In even the most unglamorous roles, you have built real leadership ability that has prepared you for bigger things.

Leadership: A Transferable Commodity

Epiphany may be a bit too dramatic a word to describe it, but not by much. I can tell you the place, the day, and the hour I received the flash of insight that charged me with courage and changed my destiny. It has been my privilege to share it with thousands of other women during the intervening years.

Before I describe that pivotal moment, allow me to briefly outline the journey that led me to that spot.

In 1989, I was a busy wife and mother—with two youngsters at home and a frequent-traveler husband who was bootstrapping a growing business. In addition to all that and an ever-changing bundle of volunteer roles, I did a little part-time marketing consulting just to keep my skills sharp and current in the business mix.

My life was full in every sense of the word.

It was in this context that a call came one day urging me to take the chairmanship of the Republican Party of Williamson County, Tennessee.

The challenge was a sobering one. Though my husband and I had been politically active as voters, volunteers, and donors, I wasn't sure I was right for the role.

Nevertheless, after some mighty soul-searching and discussion, I accepted the job. I took it because, though my days were certainly filled with meaning and purpose, I was also feeling a growing sense of concern for the cultural decay and diminishing civility I saw all around me. My children would sit with me and watch the evening news, and I often had to change the channel. *Much too harsh for young minds*, I would think. *Somebody should do something about this.* As I worked with elementary school children in enrichment programs, I witnessed the children's repetition of troubling adult behavior. I listened as the small-business owners in my community lamented their ability to stay in business because of increased taxes, regulations, and government rules.

More and more frequently, I had found myself wondering if there wasn't something I could do to make a difference. Perhaps this would provide just such an opportunity.

On top of all that, I recognized that this offer was an unanticipated open door. I had neither sought nor coveted the responsibility. But as has become more and more clear to me along the way, upon the hinges of such open doors swing our destinies. Some might call it Providence, or the unfolding of God's will. But whatever you call these doors of opportunity, I've learned to not ignore them—

even when stepping through them doesn't make perfect sense or isn't exactly what I'd planned.

So with some trepidation, I applied what I felt were my limited gifts, knowledge, and energies to the task I had been given. For me, it was all about a word my parents taught me early in life— *stewardship*. They taught me that when something is entrusted to you, it is your responsibility to do your best with it. And so I gave it my all.

In my available time, I threw myself into my new role. I had never been a county chairman of a political party before, but I had been responsible for organizing scores of programs, clubs, and events for my son and daughter. The success of these kid-centered activities invariably required the recruitment and organization of other helper moms and dads, as well as promotion, delegation, scheduling, and problem solving. I simply took what I knew about being the chairman of the homeroom mothers and applied it to building a political party organization in my county.

> I simply took what I knew about being the chairman of the homeroom mothers and applied it to building a political party organization in my county.

It worked! In two years, the number of dues-paying members in the organization grew tenfold. At the same time, we were successful in raising the overall community awareness level of the need for fiscal accountability in our government. Our team made remarkable gains, and people noticed.

On the heels of those small but meaningful successes, I was recruited to run for Congress in 1992. Once again, I wasn't completely convinced I had any business being a candidate for, much less a member of, the United States Congress. But once again, it was an open door, so I took a deep breath and stepped through to see where it might take me.

I was just one of *seven* fine candidates running to be the Republican nominee that year. Yet to the surprise of some, including me, I won the primary. I found myself in the general election vying for a seat in the U.S. House of Representatives.

As it turned out, I did not win that election. But I did ultimately see how the issues and initiatives I was able to raise during the campaign made a lasting impact with the public. And though I found that I enjoyed the experience of running for office, I doubted very much that I would ever run again. I did assume, however, that what I learned about campaigns would be put to use at some point in the future. I was correct.

Two years later, an acquaintance was planning to run for Tennessee's governorship and asked me to organize his campaign in the mid-state region. (Somehow I had gone from being pretty much a full-time wife and mother to a sought-after political strategist. And I wasn't precisely sure how!) I agreed, and he ultimately won the governor's mansion.

Immediately following the election, I found myself appointed to head the Tennessee Film, Entertainment & Music Commission, where my job was to preserve and expand Tennessee's already world-class creative content development and entertainment markets. It was an amazing and rewarding experience that gave me the opportunity to work directly with some of America's most innovative producers, directors, and creators as they brought their film, television, and music projects to Tennessee. But after a year or so, I found myself itching to get back into a realm of government where I could have a more lasting impact on the cultural and economic atmosphere of my area.

By 1998, it seemed clear that it was time to take another run at elective office—this time for an open seat in the Tennessee state Senate. With the support of my family and the hard work of an amazing team of friends, I won a three-person primary with 52 percent of the vote and the general election with 68 percent of the vote.

I spent the next four wonderful, experience-rich years working hard to represent the values and interests of the people in my district. And then that same group of family, friends, and associates who had encouraged me so strongly to run for the state Senate began to talk to me about a run for higher office.

Soon I found myself the underdog candidate for the vacant U.S. House of Representatives seat in my district. And that meant a rapid succession of long days packed with travel, speaking, listening, brunching, lunching, and generally working from sunup to long past sundown. And that brings me to that pivotal moment I mentioned at the opening of this chapter.

I was on the campaign trail, shaking hands and visiting with folks in a small West Tennessee community. On this particular day I approached a farmer having lunch at the local diner, handed him my campaign card, and asked for his vote. He took it warily and flipped it around in his hand for a bit as he scanned both sides. Then he turned his sun-weathered face toward me and gave me a long look.

Finally he spoke. "Little lady," he asked, "what qualifies *you* to serve in the United States Congress?" He spoke in a manner that suggested he found my listed political credentials and current service in the state Senate inadequate.

Without taking time to think, I heard myself giving him this answer: "Sir, I have been a choir director for three-year-olds, a homeroom mother, a homeroom mother chairman, and the Girl Scout 'cookie mom.' And frankly, anyone who can succeed in those jobs can get things done in Washington DC."

I don't think he was impressed with my answer, but it made a lasting impression on me. In that moment I realized just how much I had learned doing all those seemingly mundane jobs. An empowering truth was seared into my soul:

Leadership is a transferable commodity!

The Life You've Dreamed Of

In the years since, I have repeated that story many times.

I tell it as a personal illustration of the unconventional way many women acquire bona fide leadership skills, and how it is possible to seek and use small opportunities to build a bankable résumé of experience.

I tell it to charge with boldness women who have allowed the lack of a traditional résumé to keep them on the sidelines even as their hearts have yearned to be in the game.

I tell it to cheer on those who have already taken the first steps out of their comfortable routines and toward a place of greater impact.

I tell it for the countless women, like the four I describe in Introduction, who are haunted by questions but whose unique gifts are needed to solve the most pressing problems of our time.

Most of all, I tell it for the wavering woman in need of courage who has her very own version of that weathered, skeptical old farmer looking askance at her and asking, "What makes you think you can do this, little missy?"

I relate my story not because I think I'm exceptional—but

because I am sure I'm not. I have heard these kinds of fears and uncertainties voiced many times, and on occasion I have heard them coming out of my own mouth.

At the heart of that story and this book is a mighty truth. What I want women to know is this: *the lives they've led have amply prepared them for the life they dream of*, whether they know it or not.

Today, more than ever, the world needs leaders for jobs big and small, and women have been training for these tasks their whole lives. They can make a difference in their own lives and in our culture—and you can too. To have that impact we have to recognize that the skills we acquire through everyday experience transfer to every new task we are given. *The mundane equips us for the magnificent.*

> What I want women to know is this: *the lives they've led have amply prepared them for the life they dream of*, whether they know it or not.

This is what I mean when I say that leadership is a transferable commodity. I've seen it proven over and over.

I have seen it in the mother of three who learned the fine art of negotiating through dealing with the housepainter who messed up the living room. I am reminded of the lady at church who has demonstrated an astonishing ability to delegate as she has made Vacation Bible School an annual success for twenty years running. And I have seen it in the single woman who has learned more about writing than any college course could teach her—simply through her unpaid, labor-of-love work of creating the family newsletter every quarter. I have seen it in myself.

I suspect you've seen it in yourself too.

On the pages that follow I will talk about some insights into women, their views of themselves and their world, and their dreams of changing it. I will show you how some ordinary women turned valuable and rich life experiences into a résumé (transferring their own leadership commodities to new and exciting endeavors). You will find their stories in the "Life Equity Profiles" between each chapter. Finally, I will help you take inventory of your own skills, strengths, and passions in the hope that they might point you toward that place of influence we all need you to occupy.

The Angel in the Marble

An old story describes Michelangelo presenting a massive marble statue to the patron who had commissioned it. Michelangelo dusted the feet of a powerful figure of an angel, as the new owner admired it.

"It is magnificent," the patron declared. "Stunning! How did you do it?"

The artist replied, "I saw an angel in the marble. And I carved until I set it free."

I have met far too many women who view their lives in a similar way. The life they truly long for—one of contribution, beauty, achievement, and meaning—seems trapped within a stone-cold casing of uncertainty or fear or resistance.

On the pages that follow, I hope to chip away at that marble with you. I aim to inspire, challenge, and equip you to get your potential into motion for positive change in your life.

I want to help you set the angel free. Come along and I'll show you what I mean.

Life Equity Profile #1

TRACY HOLLAND

Custom Designing a Career

Tracy Holland took one last glance around the sumptuous new master bedroom, making sure every little detail—from the artwork to the accessories to the furniture placement—was just right. Walking over to the broad, floor-to-ceiling window, she made a tiny adjustment to the way the silk-trimmed tiebacks restrained the flowing new window treatments, which had been designed to "puddle" on the floor, just so.

In a few minutes her clients, a well-to-do couple in one of Dallas's most affluent bedroom suburbs, would be seeing their newly decorated space for the very first time. No matter how many times she had been through one of these "unveilings" during the past fifteen years, they always gave her butterflies. "What if they don't love it?" she nervously asked her helper.

"They'll love it," came the reply. "They always do. After all, you've already done every other room in this huge house and they keep bringing you back. Relax!"

But she couldn't.

The forty-five-year-old mother of three teenaged girls fussed with the dust ruffle that skirted the king-sized bed, straightened the duvet, and for the third time in ten minutes plumped the astonishing array of pillows in plush coordinating fabrics.

On this day that would culminate weeks of planning, designing, and effort, the one thing she was not nervous about was the quality and workmanship of all the gorgeous, fabric-intensive items. She knew they were well made—meticulously hand sewn to exacting standards.

She knew this because her hands had done the work—designing, cutting, sewing, and trimming each piece.

She also knew what few of her upscale clients would never suspect—that her path to becoming a busy, sought-after interior decorator had not taken her through the traditional stops of formal education, apprenticeship in a big firm, professional certification, and ultimately a full-blown launch of her own firm. Rather, Tracy's journey to fulfillment and success began at her grandmother's knee and ran through unconventional territory from there.

Tracy was six years old when she first asked her grandmother for scraps of fabric so she could make dresses for her Barbie dolls. "Do you want to learn to sew, sweetie?" her grandmother had asked. She did indeed.

By the time she started first grade, Tracy had already learned how to sketch out a design, cut out the appropriate shapes, and hand stitch the pieces together to make clothing and accessories for her dolls. A few years later she learned to use the sewing machine and took her creations to new levels—discovering in the process that she could make virtually anything, as long as she had a pattern to follow. She saved almost everything she made in those early years, hoping that someday she would have little girls to whom she could give them.

When Tracy graduated from a Dallas-area high school in 1980, it didn't surprise anyone who knew her to learn that she was planning on majoring in fashion merchandising at an East Texas university. Fashion design would have been their first guess, but her chosen major seemed close enough.

Two events in Tracy's life would bring her college years to an early close. Her parents suddenly divorced, and about the same time she came down with mononucleosis and had to drop her classes. She never went back.

She went to work in a variety of clerical jobs during the next few years—work that this creative, artistic soul hated, and for which she was not well suited. "I hadn't even bothered to take typing in school," Tracy confessed. "And there I was trying to be a secretary. I was miserable."

She eventually decided to move to Oklahoma City where her mother and fraternal twin brother were living and there met a great guy, David, at church. They fell deeply in love, were married, and within a year of their wedding were delighted to learn they were expecting a little girl.

Like a lot of young married couples with a newborn, Tracy and David had a hodgepodge of furniture from their merged apartments and no money to spend on décor. They moved this collection of odds and ends into a little five-room "shoebox" ranch-style house made of cinder blocks that had belonged to Tracy's grandparents. "You cannot imagine a house with less architectural interest or character," Tracy said.

Tracy set about transforming their home with the skills she had acquired as a girl, with no budget beyond what she could scrimp and scrape together to buy remnants at the discount fabric shop. She had never sewn interior items before, but she discovered that the skills transferred effortlessly.

Soon balloon curtains, café curtains, and other species of window treatments began to manifest around the house. If she couldn't find a pattern for what she wanted, she simply sketched it out and started cutting. In this way old sofas and chairs were slip-covered; old ottomans were given new life; multiple layers of bedding were created; headboards were cut out, padded, and covered; and pillows of every shape and size proliferated.

And then there was the baby's room, which soon looked like something out of a magazine. In fact, everything did.

Something utterly unanticipated started happening. Friends would come by for a visit, marvel at Tracy's work, and ask if they could pay her to do some things for them. Her mother's friends would come by to see the baby and the same thing would happen with them. And once she did work in the homes of others, word of mouth began to spread.

During the next five years, Tracy gave birth to two more girls *and* a full-blown home-based business success story. She stayed as busy as she chose to be and flexed her schedule around her roles as wife, mother, and church volunteer. When her husband's job moved them to Minneapolis for five years and then, full circle, back to Dallas, that process of word-of-mouth and referral repeated itself in each city.

Though she still flexes her schedule and workload around the changing needs of her family, her business has now entered a phase in which she is often making nearly all the decorating decisions and purchases in large new homes and even works with clients who are constructing new homes to help them with everything from exterior brick and rock choices to the types of drawer pulls to use.

With no degree or certification, Tracy cannot legally call herself an interior designer, though she certainly functions as one for her many clients. But she would not label herself that way, even if she could.

"I'm a seamstress," she says with easy confidence. "And I have been blessed with a good eye." She knows her grandmother would be proud to see how far those first lessons have taken the industrious little girl with a flair for design.

And all those hand-sewn Barbie clothes in mod, midsixties colors? They are the prized possessions of her teenaged daughters—girls who know that little things can lead to bigger ones. Their mom has given them a pattern to follow.

CHAPTER 2

Women and the Leadership "Disconnect"

It's hard to lead a cavalry charge if you think you look funny on a horse.

—ADLAI STEVENSON

M eredith fidgeted in her chair and tried to focus on what the speaker was saying. The hotel meeting room was packed with well-dressed, up-and-coming corporate managers like her, though a quick glance across the crowd revealed that the vast majority were men.

Each had laid down three hundred dollars to hear a presentation on "leadership strategies and secrets" from a freshly retired four-star general who was generating lots of buzz in the business community with his new book and lecture tour.

As Meredith's attention drifted out of the chandeliered ballroom and onto the heavy schedule of meetings and appointments she had lined up for the following day, the gravel-voiced general was illustrating a point by citing, at length, an ancient book called

The Art of War, by Sun Tzu, a Chinese military genius from the sixth century BC.

This wasn't the first time she had heard a reference to Sun Tzu's *The Art of War.* In corporate circles it was supposedly a must-read for everyone seeking higher levels of responsibility and achievement. Meredith had started it twice but never made it past page twenty-one.

Why am I having such a hard time relating to this stuff? she wondered. All these leadership metaphors centered on battle, conquest, domination, and victory just left her cold. Her taste in movies ran more toward *Places in the Heart* than *Braveheart.* She was drawn more to *Sense and Sensibility* than blood and guts. What energized Meredith was the challenge of pulling people together and hammering out a win-win solution—not crafting a strategy built upon a view of others as adversaries who had to be vanquished and trampled on.

If being a leader requires becoming George Patton, she thought, *maybe I'm just not cut out to be a leader.*

There is a sad but familiar reality behind Meredith's experience in the seminar. Meredith *is* a natural leader—one with amazing potential and real skills. You can't fault her for having doubts about it, though. She is typical of millions of women in our society who desire to be more and do more; who hunger for a life of greater meaning; who have all the innate tools to lead but somehow experience a *disconnect* when it comes to being the dynamic agents of change and achievement they long to become.

I'm referring to an all-too-common gap between our conception of who we are as women, and our conception of what a leader is and does. And I'm not only referring to corporate career women like Meredith. From stay-at-home moms pondering a larger volunteer role in the community to those who, as in my own story, are being encouraged to enter the political arena, our seeming inability to bridge that gap keeps us from stepping out.

I am convinced the reasons for that disconnect can be traced to two sources. Some are external—imposed by the culture. Others are internal—rising from within us as women. Thus, if we're going to make that leadership connection, if we're going to bridge the gap that keeps us from fulfilling the vital roles our times demand, we must address both sources of doubt and paralysis. Before we turn inward to examine some of the common emotional and mental reasons for the leadership disconnect, let's begin with a major barrier that exists outside of our own hearts and heads.

The Big External

Meredith's experience highlights one of the primary reasons so many women have struggled to identify with leadership as a worthy and appropriate goal. The dominant concept of leaders and leadership in American corporate culture, and in our broader society, is actually derived from an ancient and increasingly obsolete system.

For thousands of years, a society's leaders tended to emerge from the warrior class—which, of course, was almost exclusively male. The best warrior usually became the king or the ruler of the tribe. It wasn't the best administrator, planner, negotiator, implementer, or builder that rose to leadership—it was the best fighter. It wasn't the wisest, kindest, most insightful, most inspiring, or most capable to whom people looked—it was simply the man most skilled in war. In an era in which protection from other tribes was by far the highest felt need, this made sense.

As the centuries passed, even as protection from imminent attack subsided, promotion continued to favor the master general. Power was almost the exclusive domain of the military strategists who knew how to use it, focus national will, and deploy economic resources. Any list of the great leaders of the last two hundred and fifty years would be filled with successful military men, including Napoleon Bonaparte, George Washington, Andrew Jackson, Ulysses S. Grant, Charles de Gaulle, Winston Churchill, David Ben-Gurion, and Dwight Eisenhower.

This warrior-class pathway to leadership goes a long way toward explaining why leadership is still widely described in martial terms (as in the seminar Meredith attended) and why men are the people who generally find it easier to relate to such terms.

The following is just a sampling of some of the leadership books that have been published in the last few years:

- *The Challenge of Command* [1]
- *Leadership: The Warrior's Art* [2]
- *On War and Leadership: The Words of Combat Commanders from Frederick the Great to Norman Schwarzkopf* [3]
- *Leaders and Battles: The Art of Military Leadership* [4]
- *Supreme Command: Soldiers, Statesmen, and Leadership in Wartime* [5]

Many of these are fine books with important insights to offer. But given the heavy emphasis on war as a metaphor in popular literature, is it any wonder many women have pre-disqualified themselves from leadership roles? For too many and for too long, the term *strong leader* has evoked an image that is more Attila the Hun than Margaret Thatcher. (Another book to add to that list above: *The Leadership Secrets of Attila the Hun.*[6])

The prevailing concept of leadership is an image of a top-down, heavy-handed regime built upon coerced submission—one in which the leader forces his will on the people and uses them for his own economic and social advancement. What good woman—or man—would want to emulate that?

> For too many and for too long, the term *strong leader* has evoked an image that is more Attila the Hun than Margaret Thatcher.

Make no mistake about it, women can and do have warrior instincts. From ancient Britain's Queen Boudica who led the fight against the invading Romans to the pioneer American women who fought right beside their husbands, women have always been ready to defend their homes, their children, and their way of life. I have to chuckle when I think about the numerous times I've wanted to—and the few times I actually have—"gone for the jugular" on someone who verbally, emotionally, or physically threatened one of my children. We've all walked the floor, rehearsing our plan for such an attack. Nevertheless, in general, women are likely to view challenges not in terms of battle and conquest, but more in terms of collaboration, relationship, and resolution seeking.

Sure, in many ways we are still operating under that old, warrior-oriented view of leadership. But things are changing.

I believe we are currently witnessing a societal shift toward a preference for innovative thinkers who are protectors of a different sort. Increasingly we're looking for those who will fight to protect our economic freedom and well-being, who will battle corruption, and who will defend families and children. We want a brand of leadership that is more about encouraging those around us to work to their potential and to make the best better.

And on these fronts, women are as well equipped, or better so, than men.

Still, it is important to realize how the warrior view of leadership continues to color our thinking and attitudes toward leadership. It is a major external reason women disqualify themselves in advance.

The Internals

While cultural pressures and obsolete stereotypes undermine our leadership aspirations from the outside, often even more powerful disconnecting forces tend to work against us from within. When it comes to stepping up and stepping out for greater influence and impact, women are often their own worst enemies!

My friend Sylvia confided that one of her biggest obstacles to following her dreams and stepping out of her comfort zone is self-created. "Why is my mental default set on the negative?" she asked. "Why do I default to self-doubt and convince myself that I am sure to fail when I am actually likely to succeed?"

During my years of public service, I have spoken with hundreds of frustrated and disheartened women about their dreams and desires for a greater impact. Invariably I ask what is holding them back. And in the course of those conversations, some common refrains have emerged. Over and over, as women have openly shared their hearts, I have heard variations on the following themes.

1. Fear of Failure

There is a widely circulated Internet video clip of a well-known celebrity taking a turn as a runway model at a charity fashion show. She strides confidently down the runway before a room packed with the elite from the worlds of fashion and entertainment. Lightbulbs are flashing and video cameras are rolling. She makes a quick, confident turn at the end of the runway and heads back the way she came.

You know how it ends.

High heels betray their wearer in a heartless conspiracy with a slippery floor. The end result is an ungainly heap of starlet and couture on the floor amid gasps and flashing cameras. Don't we all have some imagined version of that experience filed away in our minds under "W" for "Worst Nightmare"?

This isn't scientific, but I suspect that for every woman boldly taking a whirl out on the dance floor of a new venture or area of volunteer activity, there are nine others just as gifted and able to contribute still standing along the wall with the potted plants. Why are so many of us frustrated wallflowers in the big dance of life? One of the most common causes can be summed up in a single word: *fear*.

Those fears take on a wide range of forms, including fear of rejection, fear of change or the unknown, fear of loss, and a host of other insecurities and worries. But the most common of these is simply the bad, old-fashioned fear of falling flat on your face in public.

This is why many a success-oriented seminar for women opens with a question such as, "What would you dare to try if you were absolutely guaranteed you would not fail?"

It's a good question because answering it tends to reveal both the true passions of our hearts *and* the way fear of failure keeps us from following them.

My friend Christine is a writer who chose to move to Nashville. I questioned why she opted to pick up her house and relocate. Her answer? "Nashville is a great place to fail. It is a creative community of songwriters, singers, producers, artists, and thinkers-of-creative-thoughts who constantly whip up new ideas and give them a try. If they succeed, they celebrate. If they fail, they simply start over on the next big idea."

Woody Allen said, "Eighty percent of success is showing up." The unfortunate truth is that fear of failure—and the embarrassment we imagine failing would cause—freezes far too many of us in our tracks. We can't succeed because we simply don't show up.

2. Perfectionism: Waiting for Mastery Before Stepping Out

A few years ago the Domino's Pizza Corporation commissioned a study in the UK to find out why women were so underrepresented among those seeking franchise opportunities with the company there.[7] The survey revealed that 74 percent of women had never attempted to turn their ideas into a business because they believed they lacked the ability. And more than half said they would like to own a business but didn't because they feared they would fail (see point 1 above), while more than a third admitted being frightened of making mistakes.[8]

These results concisely capture one of the primary internal reasons women don't rise to leadership opportunities—many of us are seemingly hardwired for perfectionism, and as a result we can't imagine publicly attempting something we haven't completely mastered.

Ask Rayona Sharpnack. She is a former world-champion athlete and the founder of the Institute for Women's Leadership. She has seen this phenomenon again and again and has developed some keen insights into the way it paralyzes many women.

In an interview with *Fast Company* magazine, Sharpnack related how she helps the women who attend her seminars see how illogical and self-defeating this type of perfectionism is. Her observations are worth quoting at length:

> Women in particular tend to have confidence issues. So I'll go around the room and ask people how many of them would like to have more confidence as a result of being in the class. Almost all of the hands go up. I say, "Okay, I'm going to make you a deal. I'm going to make you a counter-offer. I'm not going to promise to give you more confidence. I'm going to promise to give you more competence. And I'm going to ask you to look and see where confidence comes from." Then I ask how many of them think of confidence as a prerequisite—how many of them will do something if they feel confident enough to attempt it. All of the hands go up. Then I ask them what they are confident about in their lives and how they got to be confident about those things. Whether it's horseback riding or shipping products or developing software code, they all got confidence by doing something over and over again. "Oh, so then confidence is an aftermath, not a prerequisite? Bing, bing, bing, bing!"

> Then it hits them: They've been spending their whole

lives waiting to be confident before trying something new, when they couldn't possibly be confident until they're competent. That's transformational, because it suddenly sheds light on whole arenas of restriction and impediment that have nothing to do with anything other than the context from which they're viewing the situation or their lives or themselves.[9]

> If you wait until you're confident in your abilities and your skills before you take the leap, you never will. Acquiring mastery and confidence requires being willing to risk failure.

What a simple yet powerful insight. Confidence comes by developing competence, which only comes by trying, and yes, occasionally failing. If you wait until you're confident in your abilities before you take the leap, you never will. Acquiring mastery and confidence requires being willing to risk failure. That brings us to the next internal inhibitor of potential women leaders—

3. Aversion to Risk

Not too long ago I came across a report published by the Small Business Administration that highlighted four key characteristics of successful leaders.[10] In general, those men and women who tended to succeed at bringing change and rallying others to accomplish common goals

- were committed to their personal success,
- had a passion and ambition for their calling,

- set clear objectives for themselves and their organizations, and
- *were skilled risk takers.*

Where we women are concerned, we generally have those first three attributes in abundance. I know scores of women who are deeply committed to succeeding, burn white-hot with passion for their cause, are goal oriented and super organized, and yet are floundering because of that fourth element. They avoid risk as if it's the Ebola virus.

My experience is consistent with the findings of that SBA study. In the study we find:

> The aversion to risk impacts women far more than men—
> specifically when it comes to developing their businesses
> to their full marketplace potential. Overall, women are
> more conservative than men in making business growth
> decisions.[11]

The fact is, a wide range of studies reveals that we women are generally more risk averse than men. In finances,[12] business,[13] relationships[14]—in almost every area of life—as a group we tend to "err on the side of caution."

Frankly, some of us are exercising so much caution it's a wonder we get out of the driveway, much less change our world!

The Greek historian Herodotus wrote, "It is better by a noble boldness to run the risk of being subject to half of the evils we anticipate, than to remain in cowardly listlessness for fear of what may happen." *Noble boldness*—I like that. But allow me to translate Herodotus into twenty-first-century gal talk—"Suck it up and step out! Even if half of the bad stuff you're afraid of happens (which it won't), you'll still be better off than if you continue to stand there frozen like a deer in headlights."

In a similar vein, Wolfgang von Goethe wrote, "Whatever you do, or dream you can do, begin it. Boldness has genius, power, and magic in it."[15]

If our lives seem to lack these things—genius, power, magic—is it possible we are missing the vital element of boldness?

> "Suck it up and step out! Even if half of the bad stuff you're afraid of happens (which it won't), you'll still be better off than if you continue to stand there frozen like a deer in headlights."

4. Undervaluing Our Strengths

You have some innate, God-given strengths. We all do. A recent book on this subject defined *strengths* as "the ability to provide consistent, near-perfect performance in a given activity. This ability is a powerful, productive combination of talent, skill and knowledge."[16] You possess a whole set of such strengths, and they are as unique to you as your fingerprints.

But here's the rub—because your strengths are, by definition, things that tend to come naturally or easily for you, your tendency is to downplay them while focusing on and magnifying your weaknesses. At the same time, you probably tend to be deeply impressed by other people who possess strengths that are weaknesses for you.

If Tracy is naturally a creative thinker, details and organization may not be her strong suit. So what is she likely to do? Envy her friend Carla, who has strengths in the area of organization, and try to emulate her. All the while dismissing her creative talent as "no big deal."

In his book *StrengthsFinder 2.0*, Tom Rath calls this "a fixation on deficits" as opposed to knowing and valuing our strengths. He describes the implications of this trap:

> The reality is that a person who has always struggled with numbers is unlikely to be a great accountant or statistician. . . . This might sound like a heretical point of view for those of us who grew up believing the essential American myth that we could become anything we wanted. Yet it's clear from [our] research that each person has greater potential for success in specific areas, and the key to human development is building on who you *already are.*[17]

When I talk with women about what they do with their time, I frequently hear the word *just,* as in:

"I'm *just* a kindergarten teacher."

"I'm *just* a stay-at-home mom."

"I *just* sell real estate."

What I hear in their words and their demeanor is a discounting of the skills, knowledge, talents, and strengths that led them to that place and made them successful in it. I'm not the only one to make this observation. In a recent article, executive coach Lynn Matlock Hicks writes:

One of the things I see over and over again with women is how they undervalue their achievements and they believe that their good works will be obvious. Or, they think: this is easy and anyone with half a brain could do this. Many women do not see their key productive strengths and talents.[18]

Today, too many women are overly focused on what they are not and undervalue what they are.

5. Measuring by the Wrong Standard

Some women can't connect with the concept of themselves as leaders or positive influencers because they have bought in to a false standard of what a leader looks and acts like.

When I say "highly successful woman leader," what image comes to your mind? Is the woman you see wealthy? What is she wearing? A business suit? Does she have advanced university degrees? Is she childless? Single?

The fact is, a lot of us carry around a highly detailed mental concept of the "kind of woman"

> Isn't it ironic that we're justifiably annoyed when thoughtless men stereotype women, and yet many of us are guilty of constructing a mental caricature of how a woman who exerts positive influence looks, talks, and acts?

that is a candidate for leadership, and, to use some Middle

Tennessee vernacular, she ain't us! Isn't it ironic that we're justifiably annoyed when thoughtless men stereotype women, and yet many of us are guilty of constructing a mental caricature of how a woman who exerts positive influence looks, talks, and acts?

One day as I campaigned door-to-door, I stepped onto someone's porch, knocked on the door, and was greeted by a delightful elderly man. I introduced myself and asked for his vote. He responded by asking me to wait on the porch while he summoned his wife. I soon learned that this sweet couple had followed the fight I was leading against the introduction of a state income tax and had been on my e-mail list. Their mental picture of me had been that I was tall, dark-haired, and severe. When he saw me standing on his porch in tennis shoes—a five-foot-three-inch blonde—he was shocked. "You don't look like I thought you would," he said. "For such a big fighter, you're a little bitty thing!"

Not only do many women pre-disqualify themselves for influence simply because they don't fit the stereotype, many others discount their present level of success and achievements for the same reason. Too often we use the wrong measuring stick for success. We hold ourselves up to the wrong standard—often one presented to us by Hollywood screenwriters.

We all remember the old song "I'm a Woman" ("I can bring home the bacon *and* fry it up in the pan . . ."), but in reality none of us is going to be the superwoman that song describes. What we do know in our hearts is that there is something we do better than almost anyone else.

The truth is that for millions of us, success looks a little different than it does for many men because we operate from a different set of priorities, values, and viewpoints.

This is a truth that is very much on display in an article by

Anna Fels, MD, titled "Do Women Lack Ambition?" that appeared in *Harvard Business Review* in 2004. Dr. Fels describes her conversations with many highly accomplished and skilled women about their attitudes toward advancement and "ambition." She writes:

> The women I interviewed hated the very word. For them, "ambition" necessarily implied egotism, selfishness, self-aggrandizement, or the manipulative use of others for one's own ends. None of them would admit to being ambitious. . . . Clearly these women were caught up in some sort of fear. But of what?[19]

I believe one answer to that question is "a fear of not being perceived as feminine." In other words, they're afraid of the stereotype of the women who desire to lead.

Fels also describes how many women pursue their goals only after they've satisfied the needs of their families, including caring for children and elderly parents—certainly this is a powerful and underappreciated form of leadership in itself! And she found that women tend to underestimate their abilities and are therefore less likely to pursue lofty career goals, as I have pointed out.

Bridging the Gap

If you have longed for an opportunity for greater impact or influence but found yourself frustrated or conflicted, I suspect you identified with one or more of these, which are the most common of the reasons I have identified for the "leadership disconnect."

Now that we clearly see the gap, how do we bridge it? How can we learn to embrace leadership as a worthy and appropriate goal and then take real steps toward making that connection? This is not about a quick fix. It is about changing your self-perception. That's precisely where we're headed on this journey. Our next steps will be to directly address the disconnecting forces we've just identified.

Let's build some bridges.

Life Equity Profile #2

DIMPLES KELLOGG

A Funny Name, but She's "Got Game"

Everyone asks.

You can't help but wonder. And smile. ("Dimples? Really?")

It sounds like a stage name or nom de plume for an actor or writer intent on escaping the ubiquity of a boring name and creating a memorable brand for herself.

But for author Dimples Kellogg, a quick explanation of her honest-to-goodness given name is always graciously extended to the curious. Most assume it was a favorite childhood nickname that just stuck. But it's as authentic as the forthright woman who's been accused by friends of being willing to "argue with a sign post."

Moments after making her grand entrance into the world in 1952, her father took one look at her and proudly proclaimed that, henceforth, she would be known as "Dimples." Her mother's disdain for nicknames led to a brief postpartum discussion. She distinctly did not want to name her newborn one name and call her by another. "Fair enough," her father agreed, and proceeded to officially and forever pay tribute to the baby girl's remarkable dimples as he inked her name to the legal paperwork in the hospital.

"What's worse is that it's 'Ruby Dimples,' and they never

saw the humor in it," she said of her parents. "My grand-mother was a 'Ruby' and that's where that came from, so it was Ruby Dimples Brown. And that's how I had to go through school . . . it's cute 'til you're about five and after that . . . ," she trailed off. These days her business cards identify her as "D. B. Kellogg" in a nod toward professionalism.

Despite her mother's best efforts to make sure her daughter went through life by her true given name, it wasn't long before Dimples became known at her dad's Hot Springs, Arkansas, business as simply "Re-Pete." "My dad had this very formal name, but everyone called him 'Pete.' Because I was always with him, they all called me 'Re-Pete.'"

Through the family business of wholesaling tobacco products, candy, and school supplies, Dimples was exposed at an early age to the hard work it took to make a business succeed. As the younger of two daughters by a decade, Dimples recalled her father "raising me like a boy . . . in that it was assumed boys were more responsible." These early opportunities to shoulder responsibility laid the groundwork for the woman she would later become. "If he trusted me to do something, he just assumed it would always get done," she said. "I've noticed that a lot about women, particularly when their dad expends a little bit of interest in them and says, 'You can do it,' it seems to me that we get to be tougher."

After her father's unexpected death just before beginning her senior year in high school, Dimples's world went through a series of jarring changes. The family business was sold, and after graduation she began college close to home to be available to her mother as she adjusted to widowhood. She first pursued a teaching degree at the University of Central Arkansas and then a master's degree in literature at the University of Oklahoma.

Because teaching was an acceptable career path for many women of the South at the time, she graduated from OU with "gazillions" of other young women, all pursuing a finite number of teaching opportunities. Her first job as a sales clerk at a bookstore paid a meager three dollars per hour. Not exactly the job she envisioned when she was studying the great books of Western civilization back in college, but at least she was surrounded by books every time she reported for work.

From there she found work as a proofreader at a small print shop in Little Rock. Catching typographical errors and making sure subjects and verbs were in happy agreement was in a step slightly more aligned with her literary education and definitely more intellectually challenging than stocking bookshelves.

Before long she was married and on the move to Nashville for the sake of her husband's job. There her literature degree and proofreading experience landed her a job working as an editorial assistant on curriculum for church schools at the United Methodist Publishing House. Looking back she sees how each of these positions was good preparation for the next, but for her and most of the women of her era in the early 1970s, there was little thought given to charting a career path, determining a desired end, or even setting some short-term goals.

"We weren't that intentional," she said of herself and other women in the workforce at that time. "We just kind of took things as they came and dealt with them as they came. I definitely dealt with change out of necessity. I never planned or initiated change. I certainly never dreamed I'd end up in the publishing world. I thought I was going to be a teacher."

In that season, Dimples's career advancements could clearly be described as reactive—reactive to life's circumstances, reactive to her husband's career, reactive to the dictates of the professional world at this time. There came a time, however, when Dimples grew weary of being in the passenger seat of life and got a strong itch to drive.

This latently proactive side of her had been simmering just below the surface, and it wasn't long before it boiled over. Her final stint at working for someone else was as an editor at a major publishing house. Emboldened by experience and a thorough understanding of what it takes to make a book, Dimples informed two male executives at the company of her plans to go out on her own. Their responses floored her.

"What they said was essentially, 'Have you talked with your husband about this?' but what they meant was, 'Did you get his permission?'" Dimples said. "It wasn't, 'Have you really been thoughtful about this and thought this through?'"

Naturally she had been considerate enough to discuss this big career step with her husband and its implications for their lifestyle. But did she seek his permission? Definitely not. And was the skepticism of her former bosses a point of concern?

"No!" she said firmly. "It just made me madder and more determined to get it done and succeed."

Twenty years later, the prolific writer-editor-proofreader not only has managed to make it on her own but has truly flourished since leaving the security of a large corporation. A quick search for her name at an online bookseller's site like Amazon.com will reveal that she has written or edited scores of published books.

"Society and everything else made me a little bit more fearful to do what I thought should be done. I was reluctant to do that because, of course, you didn't want society to tell you that you couldn't do whatever it was you were contemplating."

Old societal mores have shifted, and the cautious need for approval has given way to a resolve that comes with weathering more than just a few of life's storms.

Dimples Kellogg has realized she's "got game" and feels an innate sense of obligation to use it for the benefit of all. Besides that, she's quick to cite the Bible's admonishment that to waste one's God-given talents is a sin. Among her charges to young women beginning their professional trek, she said, "I go back to the old teaching from Sunday school— whatever gifts you possess, you've got to use them . . . It's just wrong to not use your abilities to their fullest, no matter what they are."

Looking ahead to broadening her impact, Dimples eagerly eyes the future and hopes to write biographies of accomplished women, particularly women who have made an impact just by living intentionally and taking care of unmet needs.

"I'm trying to be much less fearful about stepping out and doing whatever I think needs to be done," she said.

Who knows? The next inspiring biography she writes may be her own.

CHAPTER 3

You—the Brave Risk Taker (Yes, *You!*)

> Security is mostly a superstition. It does not exist in nature, nor do the children of men as a whole experience it. Avoiding danger is no safer in the long run than outright exposure. Life is either a daring adventure or nothing.
>
> —HELEN KELLER

R emember the soul-searing questions posed by the four very different women in the Introduction of this book?

"Am I finished?"

"What if I step out and fall on my face?"

"Who will recognize what I have to offer?"

"Do I have what it takes to make a real difference?"

Look at those questions now in the light of the leadership disconnects we explored in the previous chapter. Do you see elements of risk aversion, fear of failure, undervaluing one's strengths—or any of the other internal and external forces we identified—at work here?

These women aren't alone in asking such questions. These are, in fact, surprisingly common. (Did you think you were alone?) Furthermore, these doubts represent key barriers that keep women from stepping into the places of influence and contribution our culture so vitally needs them to occupy. As we have seen, they create a mental and emotional disconnect between our aspirations and our actions. Most tragically, *they keep women from realizing that what they have done has prepared them in unseen ways for what they dream of doing.*

Let's attack those barriers. Let's make that leadership connection by exposing those shadowy doubts—one by one—to the bright light of truth and reality.

Fear of Failure—Feel It and Jump Anyway

Nancy Anderson, author of *Work with Passion*, writes, "Courage is not the absence of fear; rather it is the ability to take action in the face of fear."[1] I have certainly found that to be the case on my journey.

It seems to me that every single door of opportunity that has opened before me had in front of it not a "Welcome" mat but one labeled "Are You Crazy?!" And as if in some perverse version of Dante's *Inferno,* my fears and insecurities would invariably paint a sign above those open doors declaring, "Abandon dignity and self-respect, all ye who enter here."

At each point, I could have cited a hundred good reasons to pass. But how grateful I am that I swallowed hard and stepped through those doors anyway—that I didn't, in the words of Winston Churchill, "take counsel of my fears."

Did you know that your fears will try to counsel you? They

will. Yet their advice is almost always poor and limiting. My fears gave me encouraging counsel like:

- "Just say 'no.' There's been a mistake. You're not qualified."
- "Don't go for it! You can't handle it. This isn't a good time. You need more preparation. Maybe next year."
- "What are you thinking? You're going to make a complete mess of this, and everyone will see it, and you'll be humiliated, and no one will ever ask you to do anything again, and you'll be stuck doing the same old thing forever!" (Fears often shout their counsel in long, run-on sentences.)

Thank God I didn't follow the prescription of my own doubts and insecurities. Instead, I did something along the lines of former president Rutherford B. Hayes's advice in a letter to a friend. He wrote, "The bold enterprises are the successful ones. Take counsel of your hopes rather than of fears to win in this business."[2]

I like that. Let your hopes counsel you, not your fears.

Be bold? Yes! It's the vital ingredient if you're going to get a business license and hang out a shingle when most people doubt anyone would dare hire you to promote their retail establishment. It is what moves you forward when everyone is asking, "What makes you think you know more or are more creative or more innovative than a big agency?" Bet on hope. Don't succumb to fear.

Another key to overcoming fear of failure is to look it square in the eyes. The prospect of failing is always much more terrifying when it is allowed to lurk in the shadows—shapeless, indistinct, and menacing. There is something quite powerful and liberating about fully engaging the legitimate implications of failing. It is what some have called imagining "the worst-case scenario."

Timothy Ferriss writes about this concept at length in his book about taking bold entrepreneurial leaps in new directions. He calls it "defining your nightmare":

Define your nightmare, the absolute worst that could happen if you did what you are considering. What doubt, fears, and "what ifs" pop up as you consider the big changes you can—or need to—make? Envision them in painstaking detail. Would it be the end of your life? What would be the permanent impact, if any, on a scale of 1–10? Are these things really permanent? How likely do you think it is that they would really happen?[3]

With very few exceptions, the worst-case outcome is not nearly as perilous or permanent or probable as our fears have made it out to be. This is what the great writer George Eliot (Mary Ann Evans) had in mind when she said, "I'm proof against that word failure. I've seen behind it. The only failure a person ought to fear is failure in cleaving to the purpose one sees to be best."[4]

Hear, hear! Let's fear *that* for a change. Let's fear selling ourselves short. Let's fear leaving our highest callings un–walked-in. Let's be afraid of allowing timidity or cautiousness or the silly opinions of people who don't even really care about us to keep us from doing something of lasting value.

Here is my challenge to you. Take a pair of pliers in your delicate, feminine hands and pull the fangs out of the fear of failure that is paralyzing you and keeping you from moving into new territory. How? As I have suggested, you do that by looking the prospect of failure full in the face; realizing that even at its worst, the consequences are temporary and survivable; and then taking a step.

It probably doesn't even have to be *the* step—the full, no-turning-back plunge—just *a* step. But almost certainly one you are avoiding because it scares you. As Timothy Ferriss explains:

> Usually, what we most fear doing is what we most need to do. That phone call, that conversation, whatever the action might be—it is the fear of unknown outcomes that prevents us from doing what we need to do. Define the worst case, accept it, and do it.[5]

Here is a secret most women don't know: it's not about *being* brave; it's about *acting* bravely. As Aristotle said, "We become brave by doing brave acts." And as one prominent success consultant observed more recently, "Courage comes from acting courageously on a day-to-day basis."[6]

So, take the step.

"But isn't that sort of . . . you know . . . risky?" you may ask.

Ah yes, the risk. That was another "disconnector" on our list.

Risk Aversion—Becoming a Skilled Risk Taker

Over and over in the literature of achievement, the ability to take intelligent, calculated risks is cited as a key attribute of those who lead and do big things. Earl Nightingale, one of the original fathers of success and motivational learning, writes, "You can measure opportunity with the same yardstick that measures the risk involved. They go together."[7] And as we learned in the previous chapter, it is precisely on this point that so many women struggle. There is something about our conditioning and our wiring that tends to make our preferred modes of operation cautious, supercautious, and hypercautious.

I'm joking, of course. As individuals, women display a wide range of comfort levels with risk. I know quite a few bungee-jumping, shark-cage diving, penny-stock investing, and drop-of-the-hat job-changing ladies. But it doesn't change the reality that for a large number of women, a strong aversion to risk is a key barrier to stepping out and stepping up.

Is it possible to learn to be an intelligent risk taker? I'm no expert in human behavior, but I've read numerous credible experts who say the answer is a resounding *yes*! Furthermore, I've seen it with my own eyes in the lives of scores of women. And finally, I've seen it in my own life.

I have learned that a major key is knowing how to pick your battles and opportunities. How well I remember that as a college freshman I wanted to learn how to sell, so I accepted the challenge of selling books door-to-door. I was the only female on the sales team, but I knew I would have family and friends supporting me and the risk would be worth the reward if I managed to succeed.

In my reading and in my life experience, I have discovered a number of powerful keys for learning to embrace and manage risk. Among them are the following:

1. Embrace risk as an essential by-product of living and doing.

If you're alive on planet Earth, risk is part of the deal. In fact, a meteor could suddenly strike the spot upon which you are currently reading this book. It's unlikely in the extreme. But it's possible. (By the way, the statisticians tell us that the proverbial meteor strike is actually quite a bit *more* likely than the odds of picking the right numbers in one of the big lottery jackpots, yet people lay down hard-earned cash for a ticket every day. Go figure.)

When you think about it, exposure to risk is life affirming. That quickened pulse and those stomach butterflies are letting you know that you're alive and on the move—you're doing something, and as a result great things are possible.

2. Transform your risk paradigm.

For most women, the very word *risk* carries a bundle of hairraising connotations. Associated words like *loss, injury,* and even *death* come along for the ride when the word *risk* jumps into the passenger seat. This is something Pat Lynch, creator and editor-in-chief of *Women's Radio* magazine, identifies when she writes:

> Look up the term risk. The meaning itself does not connote a positive. *Danger, Jeopardy, Peril, Hazard.* Craft a new definition that revolves around *Possibility, Chance, Opportunity, Venture,* and *Choice.* This shift in perception has an immediate payoff.[8]

This is excellent advice. It is possible to build a new set of associations for the word *risk*—associations that are positive, exciting, and energizing. Of course, these aren't mind games. This paradigm shift is grounded in the reality that reward is very much a companion of risk. And the corollary is generally true: the greater the risks, the greater the rewards.

One woman who knows this very well is a fellow Tennessee resident named Debra. Way back in 1977, Debra was a twenty-year-old housewife with no business experience and no money to speak of. What she did have was a recipe her friends and family seemed crazy about and the idea that she could turn that recipe into a business.

To launch that idea would require money—a huge amount of it relative to her modest resources. Borrowing a large sum of money for an untried, unproven dream felt like an enormous risk. And it was. But her passion and faith in her idea was big too. So big in fact, she somehow managed to convince a bank to loan her money for the venture.

It's been thirty years now since Debra "Debbi" Fields opened her very first Mrs. Fields cookie store. Today there are more than six hundred and fifty Mrs. Fields locations in the United States and sixty-five international locations in eleven countries. She serves as both founder and chairman of a $500 million company. In a recent interview, Debbi said, "People talk about success, dream about success, and want to be successful. But to move to the next rung on the ladder, you've got to take risks. You've got to move out of your comfort zone."[9]

Obviously it is easier to embrace risk—to even welcome it—when you realize it has a companion: reward.

To make the leadership connection, we have to stop viewing risk solely in terms of loss and danger.

3. Create a "bias for action."

In their classic book *In Search of Excellence*, Tom Peters and Robert Waterman identify eight qualities that are characteristic of outstanding companies in the United States. One of them is "a bias for action," which they describe as a tendency to act rather than remain passive. The authors repeatedly use phrases such as "do it," "fix it," and "try it" and assert that chaotic action is preferable to orderly inaction.[10]

In this case what is true for corporations is equally true for individuals. Whether the path of your dreams runs through a new career, a new business, community work, politics, or ministry, you will still need a bias for action to start and continue moving down that path. This is especially true if you battle an aversion to risk.

I like what publishing pioneer Henrietta Mears said many years ago: "It's difficult to steer a parked car. So get moving."[11]

4. Cultivate an awareness of the cost of inaction.

Women who are risk averse are almost always focused on the *potential* costs of action if things should go wrong. What they almost never consider are the almost certain costs of *inaction*. And paralysis, or simply maintaining the status quo, always carries a price—just not always one that can be measured in dollars and cents.

Once again, here's serial entrepreneur Timothy Ferriss challenging us:

What is it costing you—financially, emotionally, and physically—to postpone action? . . . If you don't pursue those things that excite you, where will you be in one year, five years, and ten years? . . . If you telescope out 10 years and know with 100% certainty that it is a path of disappointment and regret, and if we define risk as "the likelihood of an irreversible negative outcome," inaction is the greatest risk of all.[12]

Don't get me wrong. Timing is important—often *very* important. But there will never be a risk-free time to step out. And you are not intelligently and rationally evaluating your risks if you are not carefully considering the downside of waiting.

Yes, inaction carries a cost. And often the price it exacts is dear. Some opportunities only come once.

5. Trade in your perfectionism.

In the previous chapter we observed that our common barriers of risk avoidance and fear of failure are often tied to another quirk—perfectionism.

It is tempting to view a tendency toward perfectionism as a wholly problematic thing. But though this attribute of temperament clearly has its "dark side" and pitfalls, if under control and in balance it's a good thing.

For example, whenever I'm zooming up to the seventieth floor of a skyscraper in an elevator, I tend to prefer that the people who installed that elevator had strong perfectionist temperaments. Or if I was going to have surgery on my eyes, I'd be just fine with my surgeon indulging her perfectionist tendencies to her heart's content. The fact is there are roles and tasks for which people with that meticulous, exacting bent are ideally suited. The problem is that most roles and tasks in life aren't eye surgery.

When perfectionism gets out of balance and becomes a dominant life habit, it is a powerful force for paralysis. Viewed through the lens of perfectionism, all action looks too risky if every imaginable factor isn't in ideal alignment. This is why an overly perfectionist mind-set is a major contributor to risk aversion. To paraphrase Voltaire, "The *perfect* is the sworn enemy of the *pretty darned good*."

There will never be a risk-free time to step out.

Conduct your own survey. Walk through the doors of any thriving small business in any town in this country and ask the owners if they waited until conditions were perfect to start their company. Most of the time you will hear that they took a chance and succeeded. Leaps of faith, embracing risk, and acting intuitively are common threads in the fight against perfection paralysis.

Okay, Marsha, you may be thinking, *you've diagnosed me. I've got a bad case of perfectionist paralysis. So what do I do to get well?* That's a fair question.

I believe the answer is in making a trade. It is possible to offer your inner perfectionist a substitute that will make her calm down long enough for you to move forward. In fact, you can offer her an irresistible two-for-one deal—excellence and incrementalism.

First, make excellence, not perfection, your goal and standard. Instead of asking yourself, *Am I prepared enough to perform perfectly in all aspects of this new role I've been offered?* ask, *Am I prepared enough to begin with an acceptable level of excellence and improve as I learn and grow in the job?* The answer to the first question will always be, *No!* The answer to the second one will usually be, *Yes,* or at least, *I think so.* And that brings us to the second part of this two-for-one offer.

Thousand-mile journeys, elephant consumption, and other popular metaphors all remind us of one truth: all overwhelmingly big things are undertaken a step or a piece at a time. Your inner perfectionist will calm down considerably if you have a plan to attain mastery of your new role incrementally—one piece at a time. The key is to have a plan. The demanding perfectionist part of you won't be satisfied with just a plan to have a plan.

As with most things, the most powerful key to conquering a problem is awareness that the problem exists. Acknowledging you have a strong perfectionist bent that contributes to an unhealthy aversion to risk is half the battle. Then offering yourself the substitute standards of excellence and incrementalism can take you the rest of the way to victory. (Unless, of course, you make a living installing elevators, doing surgery, or disarming explosives for the bomb squad—then, disregard this advice. At work let your inner perfectionist have whatever she wants!)

On to Boldness!

The message is this: You don't have to live paralyzed by timidity, fear of failure, or fear of loss. You don't have to remain locked up in the status quo by an inward compulsion to wait for the perfect time or the perfect you. You can be a bold, intelligent risk taker. Yes, you!

After her death, the following entry was found in the journal of New Zealand-born author Katherine Mansfield. In a powerful charge to no one but herself, she had written:

> Risk! Risk anything! Care no more for the opinion of others, for those voices. Do the hardest thing on earth for you. Act for yourself. Face the truth.[13]

Yes, let's do "face the truth." And I suspect it is true that you have underestimated the skills, knowledge, and inner wisdom with which your life experience up to this moment has endowed you. I believe that you don't fully appreciate all that your journey has equipped you to handle. I believe that you have been under-valued by the most consequential critic in your life—yourself.

DONNA HUFF

Voluntary Mercy

Donna Huff makes one last round through Vanderbilt-Ingram Cancer Center's patient-support area, checking carefully to make sure everything is ready for the day. She stops to welcome a new volunteer who is setting up a cart of coffee and pastries. "Remember, this is about making these families feel like there is some sense of normalcy in their lives. They're going to need a smile and a listening ear. And maybe a shoulder," she encourages.

Donna continues down the hall where she hears laughter and a high-pitched *yap*. She peeks through an open door and sees two volunteers carrying an adorable puppy—a wriggling little bundle of therapy and comfort that will soon be in the arms of a chemotherapy patient enduring the ordeal of treatment.

Within the hour, cancer patients will be arriving and with them, one or more desperately worried family members. Some patients will come for testing, some for diagnosis, and some for treatment. Donna wants to make sure that the scrubbed floors and antiseptic smell are the only reminders that this is a hospital. She looks around the reception area and can hardly believe how much more welcoming and homelike the place has become since she was a new volunteer.

Before that, she had been one of those worried family members entering a similar set of doors. Donna was twenty-eight years old when a family crisis grabbed her heart and infused it with a passion for helping others in the midst of medical crisis.

Up until that day, the mother of three young boys had made her share of trips to the emergency room for various cuts, scrapes, and falls. But this time it was not an injury that had brought them rushing to the ER doors. There was something wrong with her eighteen-month-old, Ronnie. Something profoundly wrong. Their boy was desperately ill.

Donna nervously paced as they waited for the doctor's report. Her youngest child lay a few feet away in a hospital bed, unable to move, recovering from a spinal tap. "Now make sure he does not lift his head during the next few hours," the doctor had told her. Donna nodded and thought, *I'll stay up all night if I have to.*

At 7:00 p.m., however, a matronly nurse armed with a clipboard and watch in her hand walked in the door. To the worried mother, the woman seemed expressionless, cold, and uncaring.

"Visiting hours are over," she stated in a military tone. Donna began to panic. The thought of leaving her son alone through the night in that strange room was simply more than she could bear. As she was escorted down the hall, Donna's fears, concerns, and questions burst forth in a torrent of tears.

A sleepless night at home that seemed to pass with

glacial slowness finally gave way to dawn and eventually the approach of visiting hours. The morning traffic seemed unusually heavy as Donna headed for the hospital. Didn't they know she was trying to get to her baby?

A thousand fear-laced questions vied for attention in her mind as she hurried toward her son's hospital room. *Had Ronnie awakened in the night? Did he know where he was? Was he afraid? Did he call for me and get no answer? No gentle hand of comfort? In a panic, did he move and do irreparable damage?* Each unanswered question was a slice in Donna's tattered heart.

As she approached the door, a smiling woman walked out of her son's room. "You must be his mother," she said. "He is much better. I have been with him since early this morning."

Tears of relief and gratitude flowed down Donna's face. *Who was this angel of mercy who had been so caring to her child?*

"I'm a volunteer here at the hospital," the woman said. "I work a crazy schedule, and I've found this is something meaningful I can do with my available time."

As Donna drove her recovering son home from the hospital a few days later, she couldn't stop thinking about how that loving volunteer had met her with care and compassion in her moment of deep need. By the time she made the turn on the street where she lived, she had made a life-transforming decision. Whatever else was going on in her life, she would find the time to volunteer to help people in medical crisis. Her fountain of gratitude for one who had been there for her would be directed in some way to flow to others.

Years later, Donna found herself carefully wrapping a hot pad around the casserole and placing it on the table in front of three hungry teenage boys, including sixteen-year-old Ronnie. "Okay, guys, you know the schedule. This is one of my volunteer nights at the hospital. I'll see you in the morning."

True to her promise, she had spent the previous decade being that angel of mercy who had so impacted her. Even now, after all these years, it was no drudgery. In fact, it was a joy. She simply could not imagine her life without volunteering. Nothing else brought her such satisfaction. Nothing else fueled her with more passion—not even playing the piano. And playing the piano had defined who Donna was since the age of four.

She was a natural. Everyone said so. She played so beautifully that her family encouraged her to follow that path through college where she majored in instrumental music.

After college, Donna married and taught piano at home. She was especially grateful to be able to stay involved in music even after the boys were born. It was the perfect way to work and be home with her children.

At one point, after their family moved to Nashville—the music capital of America—she briefly entertained the idea of playing the piano professionally, but that would have meant cutting way back on the time she spent volunteering in the community. She dismissed the idea. Donna had long since fallen in love with helping others.

During the next twenty years, she volunteered for the Red Cross, in hospices, in children's wards, and in cancer units. She simply could not get enough. She ultimately decided that she could spend more time at the hospital if she actually worked there. Now that her kids were grown, she had the freedom to make that kind of commitment to her passion. But then the cold water of reality hit her daydream. *Are you crazy?* Donna said to herself. *You are fifty-four years old. You have taught piano and worked as a church pianist. What skills do you have? Who would hire you?*

Not long after, she learned through the hospital volunteer director that an opening for the cancer center's Director of Family Services was about to be posted. "Bring me your résumé," she said. "I'll set up an interview for you in the morning."

Donna and her husband worked late into the night to cobble together a makeshift résumé. As she slipped the single sheet of paper into a file folder that morning, she knew it was a little unprofessional in appearance and very short on traditional qualifications, but it was all she had.

"I don't know. Is this crazy?" Donna fretted to her husband. "I don't have the right degree, and I've never had a conventional job."

"Honey, if you don't go for this opportunity, someone else surely will," he encouraged. "You can do this. But you have to strike while the iron is hot!" So with the simple résumé under her arm, she did just that.

The next morning, the woman interviewing Donna barely glanced at her paper. For the next few weeks, Donna ran a gauntlet of several such interviews. With each one, her confidence grew a little—as did her desire for the position.

The day came for what would be her seventh and final interview. When she arrived for her appointment, the interviewer, a doctor, motioned for her to sit down. "Mrs. Huff," he said, "frankly, you are not qualified for this position. You do not have the right degrees; you are not a member of the right clubs. I just cannot see this being the right situation for you."

Donna sat motionless in her chair as her mind raced. *Okay*, she said to herself. *You can start crying, agree with him, and walk out of this room with your tail between your legs; or you can tell him why you are right for this job.*

She sat up straighter in her chair, smiled, and said firmly, "Doctor, you're wrong. I may not have the right degrees, but I have the right experience. I have volunteered in settings like this for twenty-five years. I have implemented new ideas, brought about great changes, organized and led successful teams; but most of all, I have the passion it takes to make this cancer center the best institution in America to come to for medical care."

Two weeks later, there was a phone message. The job was hers.

During the next nine years, Donna worked passionately at improving the aesthetic atmosphere of the hospital. She labored tirelessly to introduce new programs that would help the patients more easily endure their illnesses and treatments. Though retired, she is proud of the work she started there.

For many years the Vanderbilt-Ingram Cancer Center's Office of Patient and Family Care Program was a model for hospitals around the country. Volunteers strolled through the reception area with a coffee cart laden with Starbucks coffee and pastries, all of which Donna had asked companies to donate every day. Behind the cart was a trained, caring volunteer ready to offer encouragement and a listening ear.

Donna's efforts brought in five thousand donated wigs from the West Coast, to be worn by patients who had lost their hair during chemo. When needed, a hairdresser was brought in to cut and style them for free. A limousine driver was available to go to the airport at any hour to pick up patients and their families, free of charge, and bring them to the hospital. Patients undergoing chemotherapy treatment had their hands massaged, their nails manicured, or their feet pedicured. They could hold a puppy during their treatments and enjoy music therapy provided by local musicians.

The passion that fueled those innovations was contagious. She coordinated a small army of trained volunteers who made the program run in world-class fashion. She also knows why they freely offered their time. They learned, as she did, that real happiness comes from helping others.

A quote from Donna's favorite writer, Albert Schweitzer, came to her mind: "One thing I know: the only ones among you who are truly happy are those who will have sought and found how to serve."

CHAPTER 4

Why We Undervalue Ourselves—and How to Stop

If you really put a small value upon yourself, rest
assured that the world will not raise your price.

—Unknown

W hy would anyone want to put my story in a book?"
Over and over, as the remarkable women whose life equity
stories I relate in between each chapter of this book were contacted for an interview, I was asked some version of the question
above. With striking consistency, even these women of accomplishment and proven talent carried an excessively modest assessment
of who they are and what they've done.

One said we should come back in two or three years when she
will have accomplished more of her goals. She didn't feel worthy
at her present level of progress. Another spent the first ten minutes
of our conversation expressing doubt that she had anything of
value or interest to contribute—and then spent the next eighty
minutes producing astonishing pearls of wisdom and personal

anecdotes laden with groundbreaking insights. A third kept stopping in midthought to ask if she was providing what I was looking for and to make sure she was meeting my expectations. (Can you say "recovering perfectionist"?)

As we learned in chapter 2, the tendency to undervalue our skills and achievements is a significant reason why so many women fail to seek or seize opportunities for leadership and influence. And as the responses of these interview subjects reveal, it's a battle with ourselves we never fully get to stop fighting.

That women as a group tend to sell themselves short is not in dispute. Countless studies have confirmed what most of us know intuitively—a powerful confluence of cultural, psychological, and even hormonal factors work together to make a lot of us less likely to appear, or be, superconfident.[1]

I have given a lot of thought and study to these issues, and yet I was surprised to see the results of a study that revealed that women were *literally* selling themselves short. I am referring to a detailed academic study of male and female sole proprietors in a service profession[2]—individuals in control of what they charge for their services—which showed that women consistently tend to charge less for their work! As one report on the study's findings puts it:

> For decades, much has been made of the fact that women overall earn less than men, something that has largely been blamed on gender discrimination. But according to a team of U.S. researchers, even when women have substantial discretion over the amounts they charge, they still end up making less. The revelation that women are underselling themselves even when they have the option not to do so is the startling conclusion of [this study].[3]

I believe the same proclivity for self-undervaluation that surfaced in this study is at work keeping great women from making much-needed leadership contributions in our society. I want to do my part to change that. But before we can stop undervaluing our skills and our contributions, we must know why it is we tend to do it.

The Unconventional Résumé Syndrome

For many of the women interviewed for this work, and for countless others across America, the key source of doubt and insecurity about their qualifications for leadership lies in the fact that they have not accumulated what they assume are the proper credentials for taking on greater responsibility. The mental résumé they carry around is not filled with degrees, certifications, and official titles. They can produce no curriculum vitae showing a steady upward climb logically leading to the next rung on the ladder.

As a result, they picture themselves as the girl who naively dares to show up at a ball in a homemade dress, finds herself among a throng of women in expensive designer gowns, and is laughed out of the ballroom.

Shattering just such a mind-set was the key result of that campaign trail "epiphany" I describe in chapter 1, and that revelation lies at the very heart of this book's premise.

I know that for the millions and millions of women who have either taken time off work or delayed beginning their careers in order to care for their families, this is a particularly acute and common worry. The result is that they shrink back from seeking or accepting roles of greater influence and impact in the realms of community volunteerism, business, or the political arena. They are petrified of being confronted with their own version of that crusty old farmer, eyeing them skeptically and asking, "What makes you think you're qualified for this role, little lady?"

I'm living proof that not only is that jaundiced stare survivable, it is also possible to be ready with a compelling, confident answer.

The Comparison Trap

As I mentioned before, it is human nature to view the things that are strengths for us as "no big deal" because they seem to come more easily to us and we have always possessed them. By the same token, we tend to be deeply impressed with those who have natural strengths in areas in which we struggle. Thus, we are simultaneously blinded to the areas in which we're powerful and hyperconscious of the areas in which we're weak. That's a sure-fire formula for self-undervaluation.

In my experience, we women in particular can spend an awful lot of time comparing ourselves to others—usually unfavorably.

My mother warned that there would always be someone who is richer, smarter, prettier, more talented, or more resourceful. But no one else is uniquely you. And the total package of "uniquely you" should be your focus. How do you best represent yourself with your combination of talents? And you can always choose to make sure there is no one in the room who works harder than you.

Whatever it is we aspire to do or be, the temptation to compare ourselves to those who are already there is natural and overwhelming. Of course, as life coach Jane Herman points out, a little comparison—balanced and in the right perspective—can be a helpful thing in learning what it takes to perform and succeed in a certain area:

> Comparing and contrasting how we do things with how others do them is a natural and effective mode of learning. The problem is that we usually mix in a good portion of "judgment" into the comparison. We latch on to the notion that there is a "right way" and a "wrong way" of thinking, being, and acting. To make matters worse, we frequently tend to believe that everyone else knows the "better way," and our skills and abilities and ways of doing things just don't measure up.
>
> When our comparisons lead to judgments and we feel we don't measure up, we unleash a downward negative spiral. Comparison with others becomes the standard by which we judge ourselves, and external validation or condemnation from others builds or destroys our feelings of self-worth.[4]

As Herman suggests, comparison becomes a trap when we start believing that any *one* type of person is the prototype for success—that there is only *one* path up the mountain.

The fact is, in almost every area of endeavor, there are many different types of people who succeed and excel, many different backgrounds that prepared them for that role, and many different paths that took them there. And yet many women pre-disqualify themselves for roles of influence, simply because they don't look like someone who is already there. For them, comparison is not a learning tool. It is a trap.

Nice Girls Don't Brag

Have you ever heard or used the phrase "shameless self-promotion" to describe the activity of someone who was advertising a noteworthy accomplishment? Implicit in the phrase is the belief that being clear and open about something you have done is something you should be ashamed of.

> Unlike many men, we just don't *do* "end-zone dances" when we score the equivalent of a touchdown at work or as volunteers.

Let's face it. Even when we are confident in our skills and proud of our accomplishments, most of us are still highly uncomfortable with the thought of "tooting our own horns." Unlike many men, we just don't *do* "end-zone dances" when we score the equivalent of a touchdown at work or as volunteers. On the contrary, we recoil in horror at the thought. But it's not just garish "look-what-I-did," "aren't-I-awesome?" high-fivey displays of bravado that we avoid. Even factual self-promotion comes hard for us.

There is a telling anecdote in Peggy Klaus's excellent book *Brag! The Art of Tooting Your Own Horn Without Blowing It* that really captures the struggle many of us have in this area:

Recently, while conducting a workshop at a major Wall Street investment bank, I asked a group of young men and women to update me on any successes they had experienced since we'd last met when we worked on crafting more compelling sales pitches.

From the back of the room, I overheard one guy

encouraging Patty, a twenty-six-year-old, perfectly coiffed junior banker to share her success story. Even though she had just landed a $10 million account, Patty seemed reluctant. With prodding from the whole group, she finally stood up. With her eyes directed toward the floor, her shoulders shaped like an orangutan's, and in a whispery voice that barely rose above the white noise of the conference room, she said:

"Oh, well, it's really nothing. It was a team effort. There was this guy who I had read about in the paper, so I wrote him and later called his assistant, who said he wanted to meet with me. I went in and told him about the services of the bank and what we could do for him. He said it sounded interesting and asked where do we go from here? And I said, well, I'll bring the portfolio manager and my senior banker with me and we'll make an appointment. So we went back in two weeks. I led off the meeting, but the senior person did most of the talking, and we got a call yesterday and he's giving us ten million dollars." And then she sat down.

I asked the group for some feedback. The fellow who had initially urged her on was flabbergasted. "Patty, what was that? You heard about this guy, you called him up, you met with him, and he gave you ten million dollars! You told it as if you had nothing to do with it. Quite frankly, you sounded like a wimp."

Patty replied, "Yeah, well, you know, a lot of people helped out. I didn't want to sound like I was bragging and taking all the credit." An Ah-Ha Moment for Patty.[5]

It is not just in corporate settings that you see this self-defeating reluctance by women to display accomplishment. I've seen similar levels of publicity shyness in school faculties, church committees, neighborhood improvement associations, and state government departments.

Why are women often more reluctant than men to broadcast the news of a personal breakthrough or hard-won victory? I think a lot of us were told early and often in our lives that bragging was "impolite." And who among us would ever want to be found guilty of a breach of manners? I also suspect part of it stems from the fact that women are generally more empathetic than men, and we are therefore more attuned to the possibility that our celebration might make someone else feel bad.

> Empathy and consideration for the feelings of others are admirable traits. But turning them into a career-crippling aversion to promoting your accomplishments and strengths does no one any good—least of all you.

Empathy and consideration for the feelings of others are admirable traits. But turning them into a career-crippling aversion to promoting your accomplishments and strengths does no one any good—least of all you.

Taking Criticism to Heart

There is yet another factor contributing to women's overall tendency to underestimate their abilities and undervalue their contributions. Research indicates that in general we are impacted by criticism to a much greater degree than are men.[6]

One study in particular showed that "women are strongly influenced by negative appraisals of their capabilities, whereas men are less responsive to the critiques of others, and often do not incorporate criticism into their self evaluations."[7] Translation: "We take negative words to heart. Men blow them off."

In a July 1999 interview on the *Today Show*, Tony DiCicco, coach of the 1999 World Cup Champion U.S. Women's National Soccer team, was asked by Matt Lauer about the differences between coaching women and men. DiCicco said it was the same in most respects, but with one noteworthy difference.

He said he learned the hard way that his female players were going to personalize every piece of general criticism or critique. For example, DiCicco said, "If I go into a room of women, I can say, 'We have some players that aren't fit' and they all think I'm talking about them individually. If I did the same thing with men, each one would go, 'Coach is right, I'm the only one fit here. The rest of these guys better get it together.' "

As DiCicco put it, "Women internalize everything." Men don't (which may explain why the men in your life don't seem to be picking up on your subtle and not-so-subtle hints for personal improvement).

I don't know anyone—male or female—who enjoys being criticized. But as the research shows, women are more likely to let it color their self-evaluations. For example, how many times have you received fifteen glowing reviews and a single harsh one—and it is the negative comment that you dwell on, stew over, and obsess about?

Our tendency to internalize criticism is just one reason

women tend to undervalue themselves. Combine it with the other factors I have listed above—our hesitance to self-promote, falling into the comparison trap, and in many cases, the lack of a conventional résumé—it is no surprise that we are dealing with a near epidemic of reluctance to step out into new dreamt-of areas.

As the title of this chapter suggests, I have some thoughts about what we can do to address these afflictions.

Myth Busting and Truth Telling

In the opening pages of this work, I declared that the life you've led has amply prepared you for the life you dream of. This issue of "life equity"—the realization that seemingly mundane, unglamorous things like being a Cub Scout den mother or volunteering to organize the annual fund-raiser for the local animal shelter endow you with very real, very marketable skills and experiences—is a critically important concept. It is so important that we will spend several chapters dealing with it in detail.

Whatever you have been doing, no matter how mundane and menial it may have seemed to you, it has allowed you to accumulate real, tangible, valuable assets. You have built up life-experience equity. In chapter 7, we will learn to identify those assets and take a "Life Equity Inventory." But for now just remember: leadership is a transferable commodity.

———

Let's attack some common myths that may reside in your thinking or in your underlying assumptions. These myths are behind those common reasons we undervalue ourselves that I outlined above.

We must replace those myths with truth, because "the truth will set you free!"

Myth 1: Opportunity, influence, and the power to bring change naturally flow to the one with the best pedigree.

It simply isn't true that opportunities to lead and bring positive change invariably go to the smartest, the richest, the best dressed, or the best qualified "on paper." In reality, true functional power tends to flow to the one who is willing to shoulder responsibility. (Remember Woody Allen's axiom: "Eighty percent of success is showing up.")

There is a growing appreciation in the world of business for something called "servant leadership." Service-based leadership was championed by the late Robert Greenleaf, but it is a concept that goes all the way back to the Bible. Jesus said we lead others by serving them.[8] Service involves more than just meeting others' needs; it involves helping them achieve their goals and realize their dreams.

Availability, willingness, and demonstrated ability to press through and get a job done often speak louder than a certification or a title.

Tenacity is a huge qualifier. Remember the story of the man who dismissed me because I didn't have the proper pedigree for public service? After I successfully led the fight against the state income tax, he called me back, apologized, and gave a campaign contribution! Showing up, working hard, and pushing forward had won his respect.

If you want to get in the game, you are probably going to have to stop waiting to be "discovered," as Lana Turner was, in a Hollywood soda shop. No, if you want your big break, you're going to have to raise your hand and say, "I'll do it!"

Myth 2: The people currently filling the role you are considering have special knowledge and ability you don't have.

If you have your heart set on designing skyscrapers and have never taken a physics course, or dream of the LPGA tour and have never swung a golf club, the above statement is not a myth—it's a reality. But for the vast majority of us who are simply pondering accepting the challenge of greater responsibility or leadership, it is indeed a myth. It is an outgrowth of that comparison trap we explored earlier in this chapter.

> If, in your own mind, you're overwhelmingly qualified for the role you're considering, your aim is too low. You need to set your sights higher.

The fact is, almost everyone learns by *doing*, improves by continuing to *do*, and becomes confident only because they *have done*. We have to stop thinking in terms of only taking on roles we're fully, completely, overwhelmingly "qualified for." If, in your own mind, you're overwhelmingly qualified for the role you're considering, your aim is too low. You need to set your sights higher.

Read the biography of almost any woman achiever, and you'll find a key moment (often several of them) when they said to themselves, *What am I doing here? I have no business being here. I'm in over my head!*

I recall the moment I sat shaking, with sweaty palms and heart pounding, right before a press conference in the early days of the fight against a state income tax. Many individuals and groups worked together to defeat that proposal, but I was one of the first ones out of the gate. As a result I found myself serving as the pointy tip of the spear. I had never led a large, grassroots initiative. I had no statewide network. But I knew I was right on the issue, and I had to figure this one out.

Frankly, that is what personal growth is all about. Without being stretched a little further than you think you can reach, there is no growth.

Myth 3: You don't have to tell your own story. Someone will step up and tell it for you.

In a perfect world (the one in that parallel universe we don't get to live in), we would never have to point to our own accomplishments. Great work would speak for itself and get noticed every time. No decision maker would ever be too busy to connect all those dots that link our contributions to a successful outcome. Others would tell our stories for us, and they would always be accurate and flattering.

As I have mentioned, that's not a world we have the option of calling home. We're stuck with this one, where meaningful accomplishments are ignored all the time, great work just sits there mute and invisible, and when someone does take it upon themselves to tell our story for us, they tell the wrong one and invariably get it wrong.

This is why the powerful "nice girls don't brag" impulse is such a big contributor to our being undervalued.

The uncomfortable truth is that it is up to you to write—and tell—your own story. As Peggy Klaus points out in *Brag!*:

> It's great if someone says something nice about you, but don't hold your breath. Although letting others do the bragging for you is one tool in your goody bag, it isn't your only tool. And it's no substitute for you. No one is going to have your interests at heart the way you do. No one will ever tell your story and get people excited about you like you can. Plus, nine times out of ten, when those to whom you report talk positively about your work to others, it's usually because there is something in it for them. Unfortunately, the accolade is often framed in such a way as to bolster them, more than you![9]

There is a compelling story buried in the daily details of your life up to this moment. Unearth it. Value it. Craft it. Tell it.

Myth 4: Everyone is going to cheer for us, every step of the way.

Sorry, but the higher up you poke your head, the more attractive a target it makes for the bitter, the jealous, and the naysayers. Unfortunately, as we've seen, we women tend to internalize criticism and allow it not only to annoy us but to actually color the way we view ourselves. It is often little comfort that—in the words of the Arab proverb—"people only throw sticks and stones at fruit-bearing trees."

The good news is, just knowing that negativity, criticism, and even outright verbal attacks invariably come to every single person who attempts to accomplish something can be helpful in handling it. Just knowing it's going to come takes the stinging element of surprise out of it.

This is something I have certainly had to learn since entering the realm of politics and government. It's pretty much an essential survival skill.

Before I ran for my first elective office, I visited with a gentleman I respected to seek his advice, counsel, and support. It was a visit that

> Sorry, but the higher up you poke your head, the more attractive a target it makes for the bitter, the jealous, and the naysayers.

left me breathless—but not in a good way. I laid out my plans to run, my philosophy of government, and my view of life. He listened. Then without pausing for a word from me, he proceeded to tell me precisely what he thought about my background (inferior), and education (lacking), work and career experience (inadequate), and demographic profile (all wrong), and then he dismissed me from his presence.

That three-buckets-of-cold-water experience helped me learn that every piece of criticism that comes your way will almost certainly fall into one of three categories: valid, invalid, and irrelevant. It can be very helpful to learn to process criticism as you do your mail—sort it while hovering over the trash can: "Junk . . . junk . . . junk . . . hmmm, not sure, I'll open that one and see . . . junk . . ."

Critical remarks that obviously fall into the second and third categories can and should be ignored. Toss 'em. Occasionally, though, one of the missives that comes your way will carry a valid observation—even if the letter carrier seems mean-spirited. It is important to remember that just because the message is harsh doesn't automatically mean it's wrong.

For the most part, though, thank your cheerleaders, ignore your critics, and allow your self-concept to be driven by your own sense of who you are and what you're called to do.

Time for a Reappraisal

If you are beginning to suspect that you have been undervaluing yourself, know that you're not alone. Often our self-appraisals are lagging far behind reality.

Imagine that you own a house that hasn't been appraised in years. It's been remodeled, repaired, improved, and expanded, but the previous appraisal was carried out years ago and doesn't reflect any of that. What would you do if you were trying to market that house?

Why, you'd get a fresh appraisal, of course! One based on present reality and future prospects—not obsolete past perceptions.

You are that house. Your valuation of yourself is almost certainly based upon a snapshot of yourself as you used to be, rather than on whom you have become. You've learned. You've grown. You've gathered wisdom, knowledge, and insight. You've done a thousand things—little and big.

Don't you think it's time for a fresh appraisal?

ELLEN MUSICK

Singing a New Tune

"I'm good enough, I'm smart enough, and doggonit, people like me."

You may recognize those words as the catchphrase of the old *Saturday Night Live* character Stuart Smalley, a wannabe motivational guru, played by Al Franken, on public access television.

Smalley was not your typical face of true inspiration, but for Ellen Musick, his kitschy, self-directed pep talk boosted her confidence during some big decisions and helped her continue to see the "glass as half full" when a wave of medical problems seemed to wash over many of those she loved. "I know it's silly," she laughed, "but it has served me well."

It's no wonder, then, that tackling a major career change at fifty was not as daunting to her as it might have been for many. Nor did she allow any grass to grow under her feet when, after retiring from a thirty-year professional singing career, she promptly enrolled in college and began taking introductory science and math classes in preparation to apply to nursing school. "It was a huge, huge decision," she recalled, "because I'd been a studio singer for thirty years and I loved it . . . *really* loved it for twenty-five of them, anyway."

You will find the melodic name "Ellen Musick" on the

liner notes of scores and scores of record albums and CDs. For three decades she was a fixture in the recording studios of Music City USA—Nashville, Tennessee.

Having outlasted most of her contemporaries, Ellen found herself still booking regular gigs but singing with people who were young enough to be her grown children. "Not that they weren't wonderful, but it just wasn't as much fun for me," she explained of the twenty-plus-years age difference. So the decision to leave what she had known all her adult life—singing for a living—was not born of necessity but was an intentional, proactive move to head off what she felt was inevitable. "I was always the oldest person in the session and I just knew that it was a matter of time before I stopped getting calls. I had seen people who just hung on and on and on . . . I wanted to quit while I still had work and before I hated doing it."

For Ellen the move from performing to nursing wasn't as much of a stretch as it seems at first glance. "I just knew that I had another career in me. I didn't know what it was, and I had been searching for about five years for what I would do next. I toyed with several different things, but I had always had this kind of insatiable curiosity about medicine, and in a period of time in which both of my parents were diagnosed with cancer, I learned that I felt very comfortable in a medical environment. Still, it was a dramatic decision because I had never been anything but a singer. My identity was sort of wrapped up in being a singer, and so it was a very big change for me."

A change? Yes. But a drastic departure from her natural affinity for helping others? Definitely not. "I knew that I had people skills, and as I was looking for what I would do next, people were always telling me, 'You *have* to interact with people whatever you do,' " she recalled.

Interaction with others came as second nature to Ellen. "When I meet people, I'm really interested in them and their story. I just have a genuine interest in other people and I think they know that . . . I wanted to do something with more meaning," she explained of her decision to pursue nursing. "Singing has meaning, and I know I sang on projects where the music touched people's lives, but I wanted to be able to do that in a different way. It's one thing to be compassionate. It's another to cultivate the skills to do more than just care— but to truly help—that's really what I wanted when I chose nursing."

Of course, deciding to pursue nursing and actually earning the degree and certification are two entirely different things. "Nursing school is very, very hard, and it's particularly hard if you're doing it in an accelerated way. And then if science isn't your background . . ." Ellen trailed off in midsentence as though the memories of labs and clinical assignments seemed to bring back a particularly challenging season. "For some of the students in my class, this was the third pass at this material, and it was brand-new for me. So I had to study really, *really* hard, which is something I didn't do the first time in college. Up to that point, I had probably only worked one other time to my ability, you know, my highest capability, but I definitely did in nursing school!"

It was during some of these times of stretching that Ellen came to appreciate the deep value and tremendous sense of accomplishment that comes from getting well outside your comfort zone and working as you've never worked before. "With singing, I was able to rely on natural talent," she shared. "But I really couldn't do that in nursing. It's not about talent; it's about knowledge and the skills. And it was very humbling to just be so *bad* at *so many things*!" So while she frequently found herself discouraged, she never conceded defeat.

This is where those Stuart Smalley affirmations became a whimsical lifeline. "I'm good enough, I'm smart enough, and doggonit, people like me" can be a healing balm when you're afraid you might fail pathophysiology.

In addition to the nasal twang of Stuart Smalley echoing in her mind, there was one other saying that helped Ellen through the hardest of school days. She caught sight of a poster featuring some advice Yoda gave Luke Skywalker in one of the *Star Wars* movies: "Do or do not. There is no 'try.'"

"That attitude carried me through school," Ellen said. "I just knew I couldn't *try* to do anything. I *had* to do it. That was the mind-set I came to rely upon."

The third pillar of inspiration and motivation for Ellen was the example of her mother. Years before, her mom had blazed the trail she was on, becoming a first-time nurse at the age of sixty-five. Looking back with admiration, Ellen said, "I think about how brave she was. So anytime I started thinking something was particularly hard, I would say, *Who are you kidding? Your mother did this when she was sixty-five years old!* and I was buoyed by that. There was a part of me that took great pride in where I came from and who I am. I thought she was amazing, but until I tried it myself, I didn't have a clue about how extraordinary it was for her to do that."

Finally, Ellen pointed with gratitude to the unwavering support she received at home. "The truth is, this was made much easier by a supportive husband and children. Gary was just incredible, taking over nearly all the household duties, including laundry, cooking, and driving the kids. And my children were amazing, never complaining even once."

These days Ellen is the primary nurse at the Vanderbilt Adult Psychiatry Outpatient Clinic and works with "the most wonderful people." The fast-paced, highly demanding workdays can, at times, make those chemistry labs and hospital clinicals of her training days seem like a cakewalk. But she wouldn't trade them for anything. To hear her speak of her days now, it's as if she's the one getting the benefit for her efforts, not her grateful patients and coworkers.

"I'm grateful every day," she said. "I get to work with psychologists, social workers, psychiatrists, nurse practitioners, researchers, and residents in the most phenomenal environment. It's just learning, learning, learning every day. My opinions are respected, and I'm invited to be a part of every learning event. It's just extraordinary!"

Ask her about other women facing similar crossroads and Ellen is eager to offer encouragement. "Understand what it is that you want, be brave enough to go after it, keep your eye on the goal, and don't look back," she counseled.

"Any time I thought, *Oh my goodness, I'm going to be fifty-three when I get out of school,* I would remind myself that I was going to be fifty-three in three years no matter what I did. If I didn't jump in and press through, I would find myself there with a lot less knowledge and without the ability to step into an exciting new career."

At midlife, Ellen Musick traded a studio microphone for a stethoscope. She made that unlikely turn because she was indeed good enough and smart enough. And doggonit, she likes what she's become.

CHAPTER 5

Reappraising Your Life— Calculating Your Equity

> Our deepest fear is not that we are inadequate.
> Our deepest fear is that we are powerful beyond
> measure. It is our light, not our darkness that most
> frightens us. We ask ourselves, who am I to be
> brilliant, gorgeous, talented, fabulous? Actually,
> who are you not to be? You are a child of God.
>
> —MARIANNE WILLIAMSON

B ack in the 1950s and early '60s, there was a popular television program called *This Is Your Life*. Host Ralph Edwards would surprise a well-known person with a bright red scrapbook and short documentary of his or her life up to that point.

Faces and voices from the past would emerge to remind the guests of what they had done that was special, memorable, or noteworthy. In rapid succession, each show's subject would get a panoramic view of the people he or she had impacted, the milestones passed, the things achieved, and the legacy left. Tears and laughter and hugs were invariably shared in abundance.

How often I have wished that the women it has been my privilege to encourage and challenge during the last few years could have a similar experience—to take twenty steps back from the mural-sized canvas of their lives at which they labor at painting up close every day and allow the real picture to emerge.

As I've described in previous chapters, so many of these ladies were unaware or at least under-aware of what they had to offer and what they were now equipped to take on. And one common contributing factor to this lack of awareness was the absence of any meaningful way to take inventory of the skills and accomplishments they've accumulated as they have risen to the daily challenges of life.

On the pages that follow, we will go through just such an inventory taking. It's important that you see more clearly and appreciate more fully *what* life has prepared you to do, and perhaps *where* you ought to consider doing it.

I challenge you to believe in the value of your own earned skills.

Seeing the Real, Marketable You

"Know thyself" is an ancient piece of advice, but it is easier quoted than done.

Isn't it interesting how we can have crystal-clear vision about our friends' and family members' abilities and shortcomings? We can cut through others' fog of confusion and ambivalence like a laser beam. We can see their unwarranted insecurities and irrational fears with ease. But when it comes to us? The hardest person in the world for any woman to be objective about is the one she sees in the mirror every day. Is that mirror true and accurate? Or is it some sort of funhouse mirror playing a trick on our eyes?

Anyone who has seen a friend or loved one battle an eating disorder is familiar with the concept of *dysmorphia*.[1] It is the strange and devastating phenomenon that causes certain people to "see" a false, highly distorted image of themselves when they look in the mirror. In the case of an anorexic, the girl standing in front of the mirror might actually be shockingly emaciated, but that's not what she sees reflected back at her. She sees a girl who is disgustingly obese and who *must* lose more weight. This gaping canyon between self-perception and reality is one of the things that is so maddening for those trying to help a loved one overcome such a disorder.

Though certainly not life threatening like an eating disorder, you could say that this tendency for women to discount themselves and their potential contributions is a bit like a dysmorphic disorder. We can stand there and look at ourselves and just not *see* what is actually there. What we think we see is much less marketable than what is actually standing there.

That term *marketable* is a key one.

While some women have a falsely low view of their abilities, many others are fairly confident that they could perform well in a desired position or opportunity, but can't imagine making a credible case for being given a shot at it. Their dysmorphia centers not on their abilities but on their résumés. This was at the heart of one of the four questions asked in the Introduction: "Who will recognize what I have to offer?"

It is to both groups that I want to offer a set of tools for becoming more objective about yourself, your capacity for leadership, and the areas in which that leadership should be applied. Not only will these tools help you see your potential more accurately, they should better equip you to make a compelling case for giving you the opportunity to apply those skills.

The Life Equity Equation

In the world of finance, *equity* is a term often used to describe the accumulated monetary value in a business or piece of property. It is a term that comes to mind when I think about the many ways women accumulate skills and experience—commodities of value that can be transferred and applied in a wide range of ways.

For the purpose of taking inventory, this life equity can usually be sorted into three categories. Add these three groups together and you have a much clearer picture of the assets you bring with you wherever you apply your efforts. The categories in this life equity equation are

1. *God-given strengths*—those things for which you have natural ability and aptitude;
2. *passions*—the things about which you get energized, including your interests and the things that naturally bring you joy; and
3. *life experiences*—the things you have done whether through your roles at work, home, family, church, or community.

These include many mundane, unglamorous duties and chores, which nonetheless build in you marketable skills. Remember: leadership is a transferable commodity. The life you have lived has equipped you to succeed in the life you dream of.

One way to view a calculation of your life equity is in the following formula:

Life Equity Equation
Strengths + Passions + Experiences = Life Equity

In the balance of this chapter, let's examine some of the ways you can assess your natural gifts and developed aptitudes. I'll point you to some tools that can help you get a more accurate feel for what you should plug into this important first part of your life equity inventory formula.

Strengths vs. Temperaments

It seems as if every time you turn around these days, someone has developed a new way to assess and categorize your personality. Clearly, we love to learn about ourselves and how we compare with others.

A quick glance at the women's interest section of any magazine stand will reveal dozens of magazines touting the latest quiz that will help you determine something about your compatibility, gullibility, flexibility, or, in the case of some magazines, your relative level of "hotness."

One personality-quiz–oriented Web site featured tests with titles such as the "Teen Movie Personality Quiz" (If you were in a teen movie, what character would you be?); the "Dating Personality Quiz"; and the "Reality TV Quiz" (What reality TV program should you be on?).[2]

Another popular site offered self-discovery quizzes such as: "What Does Your Lipstick Say About You?" "Who's Your Celebrity Soul Mate?" and, in the wake of several high-profile celebrity arrests, "Who's Your Celebrity Cell Mate?"[3]

It's all in fun, and generally quite silly.

At the same time there is a whole field of psychology devoted to more serious assessment of temperament and personality. Temperament is often confused with aptitude or strengths. Though related terms, they are not the same thing.

One of the oldest and most popular models for understanding temperament is the DISC personality types approach. In this four-quadrant model, DISC stands for Dominance, Influence, Steadiness, and Conscientiousness. Variations of the DISC profile approach have been popularized in recent years. Some versions substitute animals for the four quadrants (Lion, Otter, Golden Retriever, Beaver)[4] or colors (Red, Yellow, White, Blue).[5]

Other models include the Myers-Briggs Type Indicator (16 Types), the "Big Five" personality traits, and a host of others. And though these personality assessments can be valuable for learning about yourself and how to better interact with others, they are not exactly what I have in mind when I refer to strengths and aptitudes.

Knowing Your Strengths

When I use the term *strengths*, I mean how God, nature, and your upbringing have equipped you. What comes naturally to you? At what types of things are you built to excel? In times past we called tools designed to answer those questions good old-fashioned "aptitude tests." And *aptitude* is a good word for it. We are all more "apt" to succeed in some areas than in others. We are each also blessed with characteristics that are very real, very valuable, and yet nearly impossible to quantify on an SAT test or to display on an application form.

How do you measure a woman's tenacity? Resourcefulness? Creative problem-solving ability? Mastery of detail? These are vital qualities that neither academic testing nor the popular temperament tests are equipped to assess. You'll find women who are naturally tenacious, resourceful, or creative in all four DISC temperament groups.

With that need in mind, an entire movement in business management and career counseling has recently grown up around the concept of "strengths."

Professor Donald O. Clifton pioneered the modern strengths theory more than fifty years ago at the University of Nebraska. He identified thirty-four distinct strength areas, or themes, such as Achiever, Communication, Empathy, Futuristic, Maximizer, Restorative, Strategic, and twenty-seven others. In recent years, Professor Clifton has worked extensively with the Gallup Organization to produce a proprietary assessment test that is said to be able to determine an individual's top five areas of strength. This cluster of strengths can then be evaluated for the purposes of career placement or job assignment. In fact, many colleges and universities have begun requiring entering freshmen to take the Gallup Organization's StrengthsFinder™ test to help students plan their academic careers and to aid with vocational decisions.

The Clifton/Gallup model of strengths is far from the only assessment tool available, however. One of the most widely used approaches to determining aptitude and strengths—especially in the area of career counseling and human resources—is the Holland Vocational Personality Types model. A variation built upon the Holland Types is called Self-Directed Search, or SDS.

Both assessment tests are inexpensively available online through various sources.[6]

No one should know you better than you know yourself, so the most honest assessment should be by you about you. Here are the first questions to ask: What are your five greatest strengths? What are your five most significant weaknesses?

Perhaps you are neat and orderly and always have been. Or maybe you were blessed with an artistic eye toward the things around you. I know some naturally outgoing women who have been smiling and openhearted all of their lives. These are strengths. Some others are intelligence, helpfulness, pragmatism, physical strength or appearance, and musical ability. Take a minute and list yours below. If you really have no clue, or if you just want to know more (maybe you are curious by nature!), try one of the online tests. It will be enlightening to see if your test results vary from your assumptions or simply validate them.

A Word of Caution

Remember that strengths, by definition, are those things with which you are naturally equipped. You didn't learn them or acquire them. For that reason there is a danger in blindly emulating others who have succeeded in an area where you would like to experience success. You may hope to be the next Debbi Fields of Mrs. Fields Cookie Company—and you may very well have that potential. But her success, in part, was built upon her unique bundle of strengths.

A role model's life habits, practices, and strategies all can and should be emulated. But her strengths are her strengths. Yours are yours. Don't let this discourage you, though. As I pointed out earlier, there are many paths up the mountain. You can have an impact that is similar to that of someone you admire, with your own unique bundle of strengths. But if you are naturally a creative introvert, you can't simply *will* yourself to become a strategic extrovert, simply because your role model used those strengths on her journey.

So go ahead, acknowledge your strengths by listing them below:

1. _____

2. _____

3. _____

4. _____

5. _____

Any comprehensive inventory of your life equity must surely start with a thorough assessment of your natural strengths. You will address all the things you *love* to do (passions) and the things you know *how* to do (experiences) a little later on when we get to the other categories in the equation. But for right now, here is a vivid picture of the power of applied strengths in the story of one remarkable woman.

Tenacity, Perseverance, and Faith

Sarah Breedlove McWilliams Walker was born in 1867—two years after the end of the Civil War. Her parents were emancipated slaves scratching out a bare subsistence in rural Louisiana. Her parents had died by the time she was seven, and she was left in the care of an older sister. The girls survived by going to work in the cotton fields across the river in Vicksburg, Mississippi.

She married at fourteen (in part to escape an abusive relative), gave birth to a daughter at eighteen, and found herself a widowed mother of a toddler at twenty, when her husband died suddenly.

Sarah and her daughter then moved to St. Louis where some family members had established themselves as barbers after the war. She worked as a laundrywoman, often earning as little as $1.50 a day, and managed to pull together enough money to see that her daughter received the education Sarah never had.

Sarah was in her thirties as the new century dawned. It was about that time she contracted a scalp condition that caused her to lose much of her hair. Embarrassed by her appearance and desperate for a cure, she began to try various remedies, eventually coming across a homemade tonic created by a black woman entrepreneur, Annie Malone.

It worked. The satisfied customer became a sales agent for Malone and in 1905 moved to Denver, Colorado, married a man named Joseph Walker, changed her name to Madam C. J. Walker, and established her own hair-care product distribution business. As her company's founder, manager, and only sales representative, she gathered a suitcase full of samples and launched out on an astonishingly ambitious sales trip through the Southern and Southeastern United States. She sold door-to-door and business-to-business, gave demonstrations, and recruited representatives.

Her business flourished as she trained and deployed a small army of sales agents, moved to Indianapolis, built a factory, and over the years became America's very first black female self-made millionaire. At one point her company employed more than three thousand people—many of whom were women who would have been earning subsistence wages as laundrywomen, cooks, and domestic help were it not for the opportunities Sarah presented.

As the biography on her official Web site states:

Tenacity and perseverance, faith in herself and in God, quality products and "honest business dealings" were the elements and strategies she prescribed for aspiring entrepreneurs who requested the secret to her rags-to-riches ascent. "There is no royal flower-strewn path to success," she once commented. "And if there is, I have not found it for if I have accomplished anything in life it is because I have been willing to work hard."[7]

Sarah's story illustrates something very important about the power of a woman's strengths vigorously and boldly applied. Sarah had no advantages. No education. No family. No role models to emulate. She had very little in the way of skills or experiences that equipped her for success in business. All she had were her innate strengths—diligence, imagination, gregariousness, and drive. In her words: "I am a woman who came from the cotton fields of the South. From there I was promoted to the washtub. From there I was promoted to the cook kitchen. And from there I promoted myself into the business of manufacturing hair goods and preparations. I have built my own factory on my own ground."

Look at the last ten words of that quote: "I have built my own factory on my own ground." Imagine what it meant to her—the orphan daughter of slaves—to be able to say that.

Now I ask you: what can you accomplish as you deploy your innate strengths and God-given talents?

The answer is: much more than you have imagined, if you will deploy them in harmony with your passions and your life experiences.

HELEN WALKER

No Regrets

Sometimes in life it is a vision of the future that jolts you into taking stock and taking action. This was certainly what did it for HeLen Walker. Before she started her own company, she was often haunted by the prospect of living with the "what ifs" of life. "I kept thinking," she confessed, "that if this business venture doesn't work out, I'll be working as a waitress at Shoney's the rest of my life to pay off the debt. But then I would say to myself, *You don't want to be an eighty-year-old woman sitting on your front porch in a rocking chair thinking, I bet I could have done that.* I decided I would rather be the one sitting there knowing I gave it my best shot."

Motivated by a high-octane blend of "necessity and anger" following a divorce, HeLen took charge of her own destiny a little bit at a time, being very intentional to take the words of an old Clint Eastwood movie to heart—"adapt, improvise, and overcome." "That's one saying I use a lot," she revealed, "because it is so applicable to so many situations. I wasn't looking to achieve a great big goal somewhere out in the future. It was more like, 'What am I going to do the next few months or this year?' " After spending fourteen years as a stay-at-home mom, she was adapting and improvising as she went along, overcoming obstacles and resistance when she encountered them.

Still, the start-up days of her business, Stardust Tours—a company that offered sightseeing and luxury bus tours—presented ample opportunity for HeLen to rely on her own instincts in dealing with people and running her company. "When I started my business, I did it by assuming a lot of debt, and that was a very, very scary thing at the time," HeLen said. "And you wonder how you are ever going to make this successful and pay off the banks and pay back *all* this money."

Going in, most of the advice HeLen received was simple and to the point: "Don't do it." She was told the business was too risky. "At some point, I just chose not to listen to it and go for it," HeLen said. "You just have to be willing to fail. In some respects maybe it was a little easier because I was a woman. I don't know that I had the pressure on me to not ever, ever fail that a man does. I always felt like I could fail, regroup, and start again."

A self-described pragmatist, HeLen had to come to terms in the early days of her business with the impossible notion of maintaining a perfect score in the no-win game of people pleasing. Looking back, she can see the futility of her initial efforts at keeping *everyone* happy *all* the time, as well as her tendency to attach credibility to those nagging concerns about what "they" were saying and "they" were thinking about her behind her back.

"I paid way too much attention to what other people said or thought or my fears or perceptions of what I thought they might think," she explained. "I quickly learned that there is nothing in the world you can do to make everybody like you; it's just not going to happen. But you can command respect from almost everyone you come into contact with by the way you conduct yourself, your business, and your personal life. So I gave up worrying about being liked and made my goals more oriented toward having people respect me, and that made a major difference in the way I conducted myself and my life."

Soon after coming to terms with her own credo for conducting business, HeLen began instilling her confidence-building techniques in her employees, helping them to see themselves as she saw them. Namely, as *valuable*. "I've always been very good at helping people see how the individual job they are doing relates to the overall company and how their job has to be done well to make the company successful—getting them to be team players," said HeLen.

Growing up as the oldest child to three younger brothers and a sister, HeLen laughingly described herself as "a pretty pushy kid." She said, "I learned through trial and error in dealing with my employees that being so pushy didn't work too well for me. I found out I needed to try to have people *want* to do their job, not just *make* them do it."

It was this openness to adapting and adjusting that has made Stardust Tours an unqualified success. HeLen credits being a daily participant in her business to helping her stay on top of things financially and organizationally. Besides being actively engaged in the day-to-day operations, HeLen maintained that it was her ability to delay reward that was instrumental in keeping the cash flow where it needed to be for all operations to run smoothly. "I *had* to delay a lot of rewards. You don't just go in and start making money, money, money. I had seen others in my industry fail because they spent their profits way too soon," she said.

Ample operating profit and personal rewards soon came her way followed by a generous buy-out package as HeLen sold her "risky business," buses and all, in 1991. Since then she has maintained a brochure distribution business, had her self-designed home featured on HGTV, and successfully competed in six marathons—all after turning sixty! Her encouragement for those with fewer candles on their birth-day cakes? Three simple actions: "The first thing I would tell a person is to find the job that they would be willing to *pay* someone else to let them do and then do it to their very best ability. If you're really excited about going to work every day and wanting to do your job, it will play a great part in your success."

HeLen also contended that we all have the choice of growing wiser or simply growing older. "Choose wiser," she advised.

And lastly, she advised younger women to cultivate friends of all ages, of both sexes, and from diverse back-grounds: "Don't be one-dimensional in the feedback you get from other people and friends."

This wisdom born of experience has brought with it a fulfilling life for HeLen Walker, one she wouldn't change too much even if she could. "You know how you can call on your past experiences every time you go down a different path and it shortens the learning curve?" she asked. "I think of that old adage, 'Success breeds success,' and now I just go into things expecting to succeed. It's not *whether* I'm going to succeed or *am* I going to finish but *how* am I going to finish *and* be successful?"

Spoken like one with a few miles on her Nikes, a true marathon runner—of life.

CHAPTER 6

Finding and Fueling Your Passions

If you want the impossible done, give it to a woman on fire.

—Vickie L. Milazzo

Read a thousand stories of women who have succeeded in some realm of endeavor—whether from the worlds of business, humanitarianism, the arts, government, education, family, or any other activity to which a woman can put her hand—and you'll see an amazing level of variety in their experiences and their journeys. But among all that diversity I believe you will see at least one commonality: like Sarah Walker, whose story I told in the previous chapter, they each will have overcome great resistance—resistance from the outside as well as from within themselves.

What is it that enables a woman to press through adversity, endure hardship, shake off criticism, ignore scoffers, face her deepest fear, make huge personal sacrifices, persevere in weariness, and swim against the tide of popular opinion?

I believe the answer lies in a single word: *passion.*

Passion was the second key element in the equation for clarifying the depth and breadth of your accumulated life equity:

Strengths + *Passions* + Experiences = Life Equity

The fact is, you cannot take a complete, illuminating inventory of the assets you bring to the table, much less know with assurance where those assets should be invested, without factoring in your true and abiding passions. To do that you must know what they are, and making that determination is not always as straightforward a thing as it may first seem.

I think many of us have had our true passions and interests buried somewhere along the way. They lie dormant and stifled under layers of other stuff. Layers, perhaps, of our parents' expectations, the demands of work and family, perceived cultural biases, with a heaping jumble of fears and doubts on top.

Somewhere under all the emotional debris is the barely smoldering remnant of a fire. And it can take some real soul-searching and self-examination to excavate those embers.

When I ask women about their deep passion and true calling, I often get the distinct impression they are telling me the "right" answer—rather than the real one. I sense I'm hearing what they believe their passion *ought* to be, not what, in their heart of hearts, it truly is.

You may be one of the fortunate ones who is currently living a life that is in close harmony with your true passions—the woman with a burning to impart the gift of music to children who has found a place to teach; the one with a heart for runaway girls who coordinates a shelter to get them off the street; the math whiz with a lifelong fascination with the stars who has found a career in astrophysics; or the woman whose intense joy is to raise a large family and has the increasingly rare and special privilege of being a stay-at-home mom.

But I suspect that for every one of these women who are living a life in which their true passions are engaged and aflame, there are three who identify with my earlier description—the ones whose fire has been lost or buried and nearly extinguished.

You don't have to be an astrophysicist to know that as you calculate your life equity inventory, you are not going to get an accurate answer if you plug in the wrong element in this vital middle part of the equation.

The Roman playwright Seneca said, "A happy life is one which is in accordance with its own nature."[1]

Knowing what you're passionate about is a vital key to understanding that nature.

A Spark of "Inner Exuberance"

There is another word I could have used in place of the word *passion* above, though as a word, it is not nearly as romantic or exotic. In fact, the word feels a little old-fashioned when I say it, as if it belongs to the era of hoop skirts, bustles, and Victrolas.

I'm talking about the word *enthusiasm*. It may be a word that would have been uttered by our uncool Sunday school teacher when we were young, but Ralph Waldo Emerson was a fan of it. He said, "Nothing great was ever achieved without enthusiasm."

Enthusiasm is a combination of two Greek words meaning "infused" and "God." In other words, it describes the state of having been infused with something divine. I don't think that is far off the mark. Whenever I see someone operating in their true passion and calling, there does seem to be evidence of the divine spark about all they do and say. (Even the word *calling* suggests that we are beckoned by a Higher Power into a holy "something" for which we have been chosen.) Sheila Graham, the famous gossip columnist from the 1930s, wrote, "You can have anything you want if you want it desperately enough. You must want it with an inner exuberance that erupts through the skin and joins the energy that created the world."[2]

In the same vein, Katharine Hepburn explained her secret to success with a single word—*energy*.

Don't get the wrong idea, though. To have passion doesn't require transforming yourself into a type-A, ball-of-fire, bouncing-off-the-walls dynamo of sales if that's not who you are. Passion can manifest in quiet intensity too.

I like energy. I like enthusiasm. And I'm not ashamed to say I am passionate about my work, family, and home. A part of leadership is communicating your goals—and the process to reach them—with energy.

Identifying Your True Passions

I intentionally used the plural form of the word *passion* in the subhead above. Few of us are passionate about only one thing. We women in particular are complex and multifaceted beings. We can and do maintain multiple passions with high levels of intensity. And our passions can shift as we move through the varying seasons of life.

Nevertheless, I suspect there are a few key things central to who we are and what we are meant to be doing that remain as our highest intended passions throughout our lives. It is vital to identify what those things are.

Author and Notre Dame philosophy professor Dr. Tom Morris writes, "Self-examination is not always easy. Many of us know more about heaven and earth than we do about our own hearts. But getting to know our hearts is a task that's necessary if we want to chart out the most appropriate paths for our lives."[3]

I also like what writer Gregg Levoy has said about this question. I think his definition can help you locate and excavate those buried embers I described above. He writes:

> Passion is what we're most deeply curious about, most hungry for, will most hate to lose in life. It is the most desperate wish we need to yell down the well of our lives. It is what we pursue merely for its own sake, what we study when there are no tests to take, what we create though no one may ever see it. It makes us forget that the sun rose and set, that we have bodily functions and personal relations that could use a little tending.
>
> It is what we'd do if we weren't worried about consequences, about money, about making anybody happy but ourselves.[4]

Cheryl was a reasonably successful account executive in an advertising and marketing firm. Her job required her to stay up on the latest trends in marketing technology and strategy, so she dutifully subscribed to all the trade magazines and attended the appropriate seminars.

As I got to know her better, however, I noticed whenever she had a rare moment to read recreationally, she invariably grabbed a book on politics or public policy. When vegging out in front of the TV, she would stop for C-Span, Fox News, or the History Channel.

And she was always up to speed with the latest Internet postings on the political blogs—checking them cyclically throughout the day.

As Gregg Levoy suggested in the quote above, what she chose to "study when there are no tests to take" was public policy. Her interests and heart habits were giving off clear clues as to where her passion lay.

The same is almost certainly true for you. Here are some other keys and methods to help you identify your true passions.

Understand the difference between goals and desires.

Goal setting is an important success and leadership habit. There is power in writing down clear, measurable goals for the future, but these are not the same things as desires. And when it comes to identifying your true passions and interests, it is your heart's desires that give you away.

You may have a goal of becoming a public speaker. But behind that goal may be a desire to be heard, to influence others toward a new way of seeing things, or to move others to action or compassion. Your goal may be to learn a language, while your burning desire is to experience another culture.

It is important to realize that, sadly, most goals are never reached. Why? Because it is only desire, hunger, yes, passion that can pull us through the inertia of our own reluctance to change.

Understand the difference between desires and whims.

The presence of deep, abiding desire is often a key indicator of where our passions lie. But it is important to distinguish such desires from whims, impulses, and "passing fancies."

My grandmother would occasionally describe a person as having "a bee in her bonnet." It was a funny image, even in a day when women didn't wear bonnets anymore, but I knew what she meant. Sometimes we all get random "bees in our bonnets" about one thing or another. It can be a sudden itch for change born of boredom or monotony. It can be a "hmmm, the grass sure looks green and tasty over in that other pasture" moment. A conversation, a movie, or a television commercial can spark a sudden impulse.

These are not deep, heart desires in the sense I am describing. And they certainly are not indicators of lifelong passion.

Think back to a time when you knew no limits.

I'm referring, of course, to childhood and youth. It can sometimes be instructive to recall what we daydreamed of doing and being, back before we learned to be reasonable—back before the demands and pressures of being a grown-up started to squeeze our aspirations. This is the time before big, dumb reality wandered over and sat on our cardboard house of dreams.

Sure, most of us spent seasons of time aspiring in turn to be Pocahontas, Cinderella, Miss America, an Olympic gymnast, and a superstar singer-dancer-actress (the proverbial triple threat!) when we were girls. But often amidst those common fantasies, there were early signs of special interests. These attractions often manifested as play and make-believe.

Candace told a story of the day her father brought home one of the first portable cassette recorders to appear on the market. As an eleven-year-old she was enthralled by the ability to record her voice and then play it back. Soon she was roping her friends into recording their own radio shows complete with music, DJ commentary, commercials, news, and weather.

Candace earned a business degree in college. After graduation she bounced around between jobs but never found anything that really excited her. One day she saw a listing for a job opening for a weekend position at a local radio station. On a whim, with no formal experience or training, she applied for the job, got it, and thrived in it. It was only some time later that she mentally connected her career satisfaction with her early playtime with the cassette recorder and her love for playing "radio station."

Today she is the program director at a successful radio station in a large market and the afternoon drive-time personality on the air. Perhaps if she had been a little more attuned to her passions and interests in childhood, she could have found her true calling even earlier.

Dream lofty dreams and have great adventures. It is what we want for our kids and what we should create for ourselves.

Journal your ideas, thoughts, and feelings.

It may sound cliché, but for many people there is real power in writing things down. Neuroscientists tell us that different pathways in the brain are involved when we write down thoughts as opposed to speaking them or simply turning them over in our minds. Different centers in the brain light up when we put our thoughts on paper. And many a "eureka!" moment of insight or revelation has come through the simple discipline of journaling.

Sit down and write a letter to yourself about what it is you really want to do and be. You may be surprised to see what flows onto the paper. Make it a daily habit, even if some days you only produce a sentence or two.

Writing down your hopes, dreams, ideas, and feelings allows you to expand your thoughts. Remember: "What the mind can conceive, the heart believes, and you can achieve."[5]

The Care and Feeding of Passion

Once you have some understanding of what you truly, genuinely care deeply about—where your core interests and passions lie—the next step is to fuel those passions so they can help carry you where you need to go.

The ways to do that are as varied and individual as women themselves. You are unique. And so are the things that stoke the fire of your passions. I have only recently learned what I need to do when I sense my motivation and drive flagging.

There are, however, some things that many women find helpful in stoking the fire when the fuel seems a little damp. Among them are these strategies:

Pull away from the noisy, hectic busy-ness of the fray for a time. Often it is simply the circus atmosphere of our lives that drowns out the voice of our inner calling. A little quiet time reading an inspirational book or reviewing past journal entries can get us refocused and refired. This is a great time to allow your mind to freely imagine and mull over your mental list of what-ifs.

Review or update goals and targets. I have mentioned that desires shouldn't be confused with goals. But goals are vital nonetheless. Sometimes we simply need to put our eyes on the prize to get our excitement back. Other times we need to raise our sights because our existing goals are within our grasp and no longer inspire us. A habit I picked up from one of my mentors is to set aside time for this very thing. I sit down with my weekly calendar, my to-do lists, and my project sheets. This keeps me pointed, centered, and focused.

Step out or stretch out. Sometimes we lose our passion simply because we're not doing anything. We're talking, planning, talking about planning, and planning to talk. But passion demands and responds to action and challenge and forward progress. Remember what we learned about perfectionist tendencies and fear? There will never be a perfect time nor a risk-free time to take a step. Sometimes you just have to take a step or stretch yourself a little outside your comfort zone. Your passion will usually rise to the challenge.

Articulate Your Passions and Interests

What will you be plugging into the second part of the life equity equation? What are your passions in terms you and everyone else can understand? Write them down, working from the general to the specific.

In general terms, your passion might be the arts, children, family, the elderly, entrepreneurship, or corporate management.

In more specific terms, you might determine that you have a driving passion for "seeing the arts supported and appreciated more widely in your community."

Whatever it is, identify that fire and give it the fuel it needs to burn brightly. Then you are in a position to put the next piece of the life equity equation in place.

Life Equity Profile #6

SUSAN LEVINE

The Bridge to an Authentic Life

For Susan Levine, the Queensboro Bridge into Manhattan represented more than just the most direct route into the city from her home in Jamaica, Queens. It stood as both a literal and figurative connection to another way of life. A more authentic life. One in which the "real" Susan could finally emerge and flourish.

Ironically, it took a death to jolt her to life.

It was the early 1970s, and Susan was thirty-three years old with two children and what outwardly seemed the perfect life. "It wasn't that I was living a lie," Susan mused, "but the life I was living was the one I was *expected* to live." She worked in her father's printing and mailing business—just as expected. She had married the man everyone thought she should marry, though the marriage later ended in divorce. She dressed the way women in her position and setting were *supposed* to dress. Again, just as expected.

Two events would ultimately serve to challenge that stifling conformity. The first was the death of her mother in 1993—a woman with whom Susan had a close but complex and difficult relationship.

"When my mother died, I suddenly felt free to make some drastic changes," Susan said. "I decided I was going to write my own story. I wasn't sure what it all meant, but I just knew that in the same way my mother had cut the umbilical cord when I was born, I cut an umbilical cord when she died."

The other event was in 1974, shortly after her daughter was born, when a friend who was very successful in the travel business approached her. He pulled Susan aside and asked her a startling question, point-blank: "What are you going to do with the rest of your life?"

Susan responded with a mixture of surprise and bewilderment. She had never really thought about it. After all, she *seemed* fulfilled.

"Well, I've watched you," he continued. "I've seen how great you are with people. You have something special, and I believe you could become an extraordinary travel agent. If you want to add something to your life, all you have to do is drive into Manhattan to talk to me. Here's my card."

"It's odd," Susan confided. "I was a thirty-something woman, but as I drove across the bridge for that meeting, I felt like an independent grown-up for the first time in my life."

That meeting launched a successful career that would ultimately lead to owning a travel agency. More importantly, it represented the first step toward the realization that there was a capable, competent, dynamic woman beneath the layers of personas she had developed in three-plus decades of being what others expected her to be.

Thirty-three years later, with an ever-expanding portfolio of devoted clients, Susan attributed her longevity in the industry to three primary things: her ability as a listener, complete honesty, and the fact that "being a woman allows me to use my brain and my heart simultaneously." The fact that many of her newer, younger clients call her "mom" is a testament to the care she extends to them continually in this highly competitive business.

"I never want to sit back and rest on my laurels. The guiding philosophy for my business is that I want my last success to open the door for my next challenge," Susan said.

Susan quite unexpectedly met the man whom she considered to be her "soul mate." She said, "We took a bold step together, and we were together 24/7 from then on and thriving on being together in a beautiful world which we created for ourselves. Our home was our nest and was filled with love. This unique relationship lasted twelve years until he lost his seven-month battle with cancer."

The grief that enveloped Susan was all consuming for quite some time. "As I was rising from the depths of grieving, it occurred to me that if I could remember the pain as well as what brought me hope and strength in the midst of it, then it would all be worthwhile because I could then help others who will ultimately go through the same pain," she said.

When younger women who admire her success ask for advice these days, she boldly challenges, "Believe in yourself, be proactive not reactive, take hold of that which is important, learn it, know it, and be your own best friend. Believe in yourself completely."

In terms of her life, Susan takes her own advice to heart: "If I don't feel satisfied within, or I'm disappointed in myself or feel I've given less than my best, no one else's words of praise can make me feel better. My self-discovery and ever-growing strength is an exhilarating work in progress bringing tremendous enlightenment along the way, as a woman, a mother, and a human being."

She pointed me to a favorite saying—the words of first-century holy man Rabbi Hillel:

"If I am not my self, who is?

If not now, when?"

CHAPTER 7

The Life You've Lived: Discovering the Hidden Value of Your Experience

> Not all learning comes from books. You have to live a lot.
>
> —Loretta Lynn

The billboard headline caught my eye as I headed down the freeway. It was promoting a local college's degree programs for working adults who can only attend classes on evenings and weekends. The vividly colored artwork proclaimed:

"Credit for Life Experience"

I couldn't help but smile when I saw it. At that moment it occurred to me that those four words captured precisely what I had asked for in that West Tennessee diner in my pivotal conversation with that skeptical farmer.

I wanted credit for all the things I had managed as a mom— for the fund-raising drives that actually raised more funds than we parents had to spend in putting them on; the preschooler outings in which no kids were lost and hardly any were injured (none seriously, anyway!); the successful church programs and productions carried out under circumstances that would have made Cecil B. DeMille weep in despair; and for all those times I found a way to bring some order and direction out of sugar-fueled chaos. I wanted credit for all those projects at school, church, and women's club I had seen through to completion. I wanted credit for the hard-fought but unsung little victories I had been a part of as a volunteer in my community.

"I deserve credit for life experience" is essentially what I tried to tell that sun-weathered gentleman. I know that now. But I'm not sure if, up until that moment, even *I* had given myself proper credit for all that I had learned and lived.

I believe it is time we offer ourselves "credit for life experience" and confidently expect others to offer it too.

Perhaps I had bought into one of the dominant fallacies of the twentieth-century mind-set—one that says an accomplishment isn't real if it's not achieved in association with a paycheck, and that victories don't count if they're won in a jogging suit rather than a business suit. Perhaps you have bought into this myth too.

I have learned that I was not alone in having accepted those falsehoods as true. I now know that our nation is filled, shore-to-shore, with untapped riches in human resources—women with dreams and ideas and solutions—yet held back by an invisible hand of self-doubt.

I believe it is time we offer ourselves "credit for life experience" and confidently expect others to offer it too.

Experience is the third vital element in that life equity equation we have been building over the last few chapters:

$$Strengths + Passions + Experience = Life\ Equity$$

We have seen the value of our innate, God-given strengths and some ways to more clearly identify what they are. We have observed the powerful roles passions and interests play in giving us the fuel to overcome adversity and the resistance of our own self-doubt. And now it is time to explore the bold declarations I made in the opening paragraphs of this work:

The life you have lived has amply prepared you for the life you dream of.

The mundane has prepared you for the magnificent.

Leadership is indeed a transferable commodity.

Women on the Alternative Path

As we have seen in previous chapters, all too often we choose to be oblivious to our own strengths. Familiarity and insecurity work together to obscure the treasures—the "diamonds in the rough" we hold in our very own hands. Increasingly, though, there are signs that savvy companies and organizations are recognizing what women without conventional résumés, and those with gaps in their résumés due to family responsibilities, have to offer.

For example, a 2006 article in the *Wall Street Journal*'s "Career Journal" reported that several of the nation's elite business schools were beginning to focus some of their recruiting efforts on stay-at-home moms:

Seeking to tap a pool of professionals who are of increasing interest to employers, Harvard, Dartmouth, and other

graduate business programs are launching executive-edu-
cation courses geared toward women who have put their
careers on hold to raise families and are ready to return to
the professional world.[1]

Of course, it isn't only stay-at-home moms and women who
for family reasons have taken a break from a career who need to be
able to take an accurate inventory of their skills and experiences.
Nor is the world of work the only place women can look to apply
them. This need also exists for women in a corporate setting looking to advance, for entrepreneurs trying to raise venture capital,
and as I personally discovered, for women entering the realm of
public service—whether it be the school board, the city council, a
government agency, or the U.S. Congress.

A personal passion of mine—the driving force behind this
book—is to see women step into places of leadership and influence in *every* area of our society. The women whose stories opened
this book and the stories of those I have shared in between each
chapter reflect this diversity of situation and vision. Despite the
differences, the commonality is the desire to lead—to influence,
to make a difference. At the end of the day, they want to know that
what they can contribute to society has real value. And whether
they realize it or not, they have the capacity.

I know that not everyone chooses to travel a corporate path.
Not everyone takes a direct, unbroken path to her desired role or
dream job. Many women are like me. They have to build their
résumés by looking for open doors and using those opportunities
to learn—to build the skill muscle that enables them to perform
beyond expectations when the opportunity comes. And though I
believe all women will find the following tools beneficial, I have

found it is these women who may have been out of the traditional workforce for a while who are most in need of (1) an understanding that they have indeed built a marketable and bankable résumé of experience and (2) a way to inventory and articulate those assets.

For those women who have spent years rearing a family, following an alternative career path, or working in the volunteer sector, it is important to realize that each and every one of the skills they have developed is a marketable commodity.

Before we begin the exploratory process of identifying and organizing your hard-earned bundle of leadership skills and assets, we need a better sense of what it is we're actually looking for. What coveted, marketable, empowering skills lie behind those seemingly run-of-the-mill experiences that may have comprised our daily lives up to this point?

The Skills and Tools of Leaders

In her insightful book *If You've Raised Kids, You Can Manage Anything*, author Ann Crittenden declares, "The difference between being a parent and managing adults is not all that different. Motherhood is truly complex and highly skilled. . . . Women have always known this on some level. For eons, they have understood that the skills, the organization, and the sheer character it takes to manage a family are relevant to coping with other challenges in life."[2]

Her book makes a compelling case for the very thing I've said each time I have had the opportunity to speak to a group of women during the last few years—namely, that leadership is a transferable commodity. Specifically, Crittenden focused on parenting skills and how they are surprisingly transferable to the workplace, and on the truth that many of the universal lessons of leadership can be learned from leading children.

As a parent and a former volunteer director of a children's choir, I can wholeheartedly attest to the truth of those claims. Working with a preschool church choir on Wednesday nights, I quickly learned that it took our entire team to accomplish the goal. One would direct, one would discipline, and one would engineer. By the time we reached the end of the hour, we were ready to hand our happy, smiling children back to their parents and close up shop for the week. But you do learn a lot by dealing with thirty wee ones every week.

You've done the same thing when you've taught a class or been the homeroom mother or coached the T-ball team. Those are the same skills, though packaged differently, that are used in businesses or organizations. A team moves you forward more quickly than trying to fly solo. In building a team, remember to focus on your strengths and find individuals who have strengths that are your weaknesses.

I have already described my "eureka!" moment to you—that encounter on the campaign trail that caused me to really see how valuable and valid my experiences as a mother and volunteer had been. Ann Crittenden had a similar flash of insight:

My own "ah-ha!" moment came soon after my son was born in 1982. I was busily devouring baby books, and noticed an uncanny resemblance between the advice found in many books on parenting and the material in books on management that I had read as a business reporter. I wondered if the how-to books aimed at new mothers and the how-to books aimed at aspiring executives could in fact be the same material, packaged differently for different audiences.

I pursued this hunch a few years later by signing up to attend a three-day seminar at Harvard called "Dealing with Difficult People and Difficult Situations." The course was taught by William Ury, co-author of *Getting to Yes*, the bestselling business book of all time. And, sure enough, the management tips that the assembled business executives and military officers were paying almost two thousand dollars per head to hear were largely the same lessons anyone could read by picking up a ten-dollar paperback on parenting.[3]

Crittenden later learned that although Ury had cited books like Sun Tzu's *The Art of War* and Prussian military strategist Carl von Clausewitz's *On War* to illustrate his points to the mostly male Harvard audience, he later confided with good-humored transparency that he had indeed received many of his insights from a famous book on parenting!

With obvious amusement, Crittenden points out that these high-powered business achievers who were "thinking they were learning how to apply the lessons of the battlefield to the modern organization, were in fact learning the lessons of child psychology that mothers had been applying at home for decades."[4]

Anyone who tried to get anything accomplished in an organization will identify with these common parental challenges:

- Dealing with someone throwing a temper tantrum
- Mediating a conflict between two childish people
- Teaching something to someone who thinks he or she already knows everything
- Motivating by reward

(Just to name a few.)

The recognition that women who have successfully run a household possess the skills to run just about anything is not a twenty-first-century revelation. Back in the mid-nineteenth century, in a widely read book entitled *A Treatise on Domestic Economy, for the Use of Young Ladies at Home and at School*, Catharine Beecher wrote that "no statesman, at the head of a nation's affairs, had more frequent calls for wisdom, firmness, tact, discrimination, prudence, and versatility of talent, than such a woman."[5]

Of course, whenever you use the term *skills* in relationship to an organizational role, job position, or leadership post, the mind immediately jumps to traditional, tangible abilities such as computer proficiency or knowledge of specialized processes. But the skills most organizations find in short supply are those that are harder to measure. Though intangible, they are the ones that usually determine success or failure in a role. And it is just such skills that women accumulate in life but overlook when it comes time to market themselves.

Once you list and define some of these skills, you'll be ready to start taking inventory of your life experiences with these firmly in mind. In fact, put a check mark by the description that seems to fit your personal skill set.

Organizing

People with this skill have developed the ability to bring order out of chaos. Kathy Peel, the creator of *The Family Manager* book series, has built an entire business out of helping people organize their lives, families, and homes.

In a Washington DC newspaper, I noticed that a political organization was advertising a job opening. They were looking for applicants with "good organizational skills and the ability to perform many tasks simultaneously." The ad basically described most of the mothers of small children I know.

Multitasking

This is an area in which it is universally recognized that women are generally more proficient than men. A lot of studies have borne it out. And recent breakthroughs in brain science have helped us understand why it is so. Nevertheless, some women take this natural ability to amazing levels. And few jobs on earth give a woman an opportunity to hone her multitasking skills like being a mom.

As Ann Crittenden rightly points out:

> A rundown of all the things most [moms] have to do could never be fit into a seven-second sound bite in response to the question, "And what do you do?" Ric Edelman, a financial services executive in Fairfax, Virginia, has calculated that *mothers' responsibilities include components of at least seventeen different professions,* making mothers, along with chief executives, the last non-specialized generalists in the skilled work force.[6] (emphasis added)

I think it was the homemaker's ability to juggle multiple projects and keep them all moving forward that Margaret Thatcher had in mind when she uttered her now famous quote: "If you want something *said,* ask a man. If you want something *done,* ask a woman."

Rallying

This is the knowledge and gifting required to excite a dispa-
rate, distracted, tired group of people about accomplishing a goal.
And what a powerful and valuable gift it is to any organization.

Some of the ladies who have been key volunteer coordinators
in my previous election campaigns were a wonder to behold when
it came to "rallying the troops." Even when things didn't seem to be
going our way, they would always find a way to pump up the team's
spirits and reinvigorate the effort. And where did they develop
these amazing motivation skills? Not in graduate school. Not by
becoming vice president of sales at a Fortune 500 company.

Their proficiency had come from volunteering as cabin coun-
selors at church camps, getting small armies of Girl Scouts out
selling mountains of cookies, and firing up the homeowners' association for the annual cleanup and garage sale. They are more than
able cheerleaders—they are coaches and psychologists too.

My thirty-something daughter is one of the best at rallying the
troops. She is a pro at getting people to pull together to achieve a goal.
The events she produces are nothing short of spectacular. She corrals
her young friends; gets them to buy into her goal for a charity; then
divides them into teams to seek auction items, secure donations,
and arrange the catering and decorations. She rallies the troops and
cheers them constantly so that everyone shares in the success of a
well-planned and staged event—the true epitome of a team.

Executing/Facilitating

Some of the women who are the most brilliant at formulating
an effective plan of action (strategizing) are close to helpless when

it comes to actually carrying that plan out. (It's a right brain / left brain thing, I suspect.) That's where those who have developed the skill of executing truly shine. They know how to manage the details and have learned the art of "getting things done."

Such facilitators are rare commodities and are highly sought after in the worlds of business, politics, and the nonprofit sector. Yet it has been my experience that our communities and churches are filled with them! These are the key go-to people in countless little organizations and clubs across America. They have come by their skill the old-fashioned way. Time and again someone in leadership delegated a task to them, and they rolled up their sleeves and "got her done."

Negotiating

An ever-present feature in the airlines' in-flight magazines is an ad that declares, "You don't get what you deserve, you get what you negotiate." The fact that this ad never stops appearing is a clear indicator that businesses are always looking for people who are skilled at negotiation.

In my time on Capitol Hill, I've been in on some pretty tough negotiations and seen the very best in action. But I know some equally tough deal makers who are soccer moms back home in Tennessee. They developed their skill dealing with people like the contractor hired to remodel the bathroom and most of all through the daily demands of the ongoing negotiation known as parenting. (Anyone who has ever come up against a four-year-old doggedly determined to wear a tutu, cowboy boots, and a rainbow wig to church knows what I'm talking about!)

Though many women are reluctant to engage in tough negotiation because it violates their strongly ingrained concepts of "niceness" and "politeness" (one study showed that men were eight times more likely than women to negotiate a starting salary at a new job[7]), those women who *have* developed negotiating skills tend to be very good at it and approach the task differently than most men.

Instead of viewing a negotiation as a modern form of single combat where one party will be the victor and the other the vanquished, women—employing their generally superior empathy, intuitiveness, and emotional intelligence—can discern what the person across the table *really* wants and view successful negotiation in terms of the highly prized win-win.

A woman with such skills would be a powerful asset in any business.

Crisis Managing

Is there a group of people on earth more accustomed to handling crises than mothers? Not to minimize their heroism, but firefighters deal with long stretches of monotony in between their calls to respond to an emergency. Moms pretty much have the inverse—a few blessed uneventful stretches in between a chain of minor emergencies. As Ann Crittenden describes it, mothers routinely deal with "accidents, fires, floods, auto accidents/repair, thefts, insect infestations, and calls from the school principal."[8]

In all seriousness, when I think of the many women I know who have developed the ability to remain calm in the midst of turmoil—who actually seem to flourish under intense pressure situations—I think of the lady who came to be known as "the unsinkable Molly Brown."

Brown was a passenger on the maiden voyage of the *Titanic* and, as one encyclopedia describes it:

> She helped many others to the lifeboats before being forced into one herself. Once on the water, she demanded that women be allowed to row as well as men; she and the other women in Lifeboat No. 6 worked together to row and keep spirits up despite the alleged panic and gloom of Quartermaster Robert Hichens. After being rescued by the RMS *Carpathia*, Brown helped prepare lists of those who had been rescued, acted as an interpreter for other survivors, and headed the *Titanic* Survivors' Committee.[9]

Every organization needs some Molly Browns—women whose life experiences have given them unexpected skills in managing a crisis.

Making Over

Don't we love makeovers? We can't seem to get enough of them. Oprah's most highly rated and popular episodes tend to be those in which she pulls women out of the audience for a professional, head-to-toe transformation. Shows like *What Not to Wear,* *"How Do I Look?"* and *10 Years Younger* get consistently strong ratings among women. And it isn't just people we love to see get the Cinderella's-fairy-godmother treatment. We seemingly have an insatiable appetite for seeing rooms and entire homes go from sad to stunning on networks such as HGTV and TLC as these networks fill their schedules with variations on this theme.

"Improvers" often struggle when they must create things from scratch, but have an amazing ability to turn what exists from frightening to fabulous. An alchemistlike ability to turn sows' ears into silk purses is a skill some women have developed—usually in conjunction with a natural creative talent.

Again, my daughter, Mary Morgan, tops the chart. She is organized, calms chaos, and turns disasters into delights when she encounters off-kilter events and fashion faux pas. She calls these situations her "projects," and I have listened in on many conversations when she has coached her friends from frumpy to fashionable outfits and dull to delightful table settings. Watching her transact "style fusion," as she terms it, is a lesson in how to organize a plan for improvement that yields a successful outcome.

Networking/Connecting

I have a number of ladies in my life who love to function as "connectors." By that I mean that they take great joy in connecting people who ought to know each other but don't, or connecting a key person with a key organization. And they're good at it. (Southern women are connectors by birthright. I honestly believe this skill comes preprogrammed in Southern genes!)

LaRawn Scafe Rhea is just such a connector. If you were to meet her, she would take a great interest in you and very quickly learn your interests and goals. Soon you would hear her say something like, "Oh, do you know so-and-so? She has some of the very things you're looking for. Here's her number!" Or you might hear, "Have you heard about the XYZ organization? They are working on some of the same issues you are interested in, but from a different angle. Come with me and I'll introduce you to their president. You'll love her . . ."

Networkers and connectors are like matchmakers, but not for romance (although they can't resist trying to fix people up if they can). While many men function as networkers and connectors, the very best I have encountered are invariably women.

Businesses and large organizations can benefit greatly by having a connector or two in a position of influence. And though they may not know it, they can be found in large numbers among the mothers and homemakers who, like LaRawn, labor among the volunteer organizations in every community. Business development *is* networking and connecting.

Promoting

Political campaigns are a giant exercise in promotion. Word must be spread, awareness raised, and positive buzz generated. Betsy wanted to run for city commission, so she grabbed the gals in the neighborhood and did what she was good at doing: building a team to attack a problem. She won.

Someone who successfully promoted the clothing drive for the women's shelter every year for the past eight has learned some things about getting the word out. She has developed grassroots and Net root networks that have the ability to activate and inform hundreds at the click of the mouse.

I am reminded of a woman in Little Rock, Arkansas, who had always done her part as a volunteer in the community. But when Hurricane Katrina brought thousands of displaced families and individuals to her city, Joy Cameron stepped up in a big way.

Cameron organized and promoted a program to feed evacuees from the Gulf Coast who relocated to north Little Rock in temporary housing. She convinced a local senior center to provide banquet space and enlisted the help of volunteers from no fewer than forty-five churches and community organizations to assist with meal preparation and service. The program ran like a Swiss watch for an entire month and served close to ten thousand meals. In addition, evacuees were provided hygiene items, water, and clothing, which were donated by churches, local businesses, and individuals. In 2006, Joy Cameron received the President's Volunteer Service Award from President Bush.

Give a seasoned promoter a telephone and a list, and get out of the way.

Mentoring/Coaching

Mentoring and life coaching are increasingly popular topics among professional women—and rightly so. As we'll see in a later chapter, finding an appropriate mentor is a powerful strategy for women seeking to step into greater realms of influence and leadership.

What consistently surprises me, though, is the numbers of women who are actually functioning as outstanding mentors and coaches but don't realize it. They are mentors unaware!

Women by and large are naturally inclusive, supportive, and nurturing. Thus it is not surprising to see women with practical experience, who have achieved some measure of success, offer a hand of guidance and encouragement to those who are just starting out. They may not think of themselves as mentors, but that is precisely the skill they have developed.

Several years ago my friend Becky gave me a lovely needle-point piece that carried the words: "Flowers leave some of their fragrance in the hand that bestows them." What a great reminder that mentoring—lifting, supporting, and encouraging people to be free to achieve their potential—not only benefits those who are helped but makes the helper a stronger leader in the process.

Arranging

Many large corporations hire efficiency consultants. These are people who look at all the complex processes and outputs in the organization and help them reorder and rearrange things for maximum efficiency. People with this skill are highly sought after.

Would you like to guess where many companies are learning to look for people with this knack? Savvy organizations are discovering that women with children at home are much more likely to have learned to be efficient "arrangers."

One report on efficiency described how large corporations were making this discovery. For example:

> At Kentucky Fried Chicken, so many women with children are good at structuring this kind of workflow that there is a name for them: *arrangers*. "We tend to be list-makers and schedulers and arrangers," says Cheryl Bachelder, KFC's former CEO. "This always comes out on strength-finder tests." She cites the example of one woman executive who loves to draw up the flow charts showing what steps have to happen next, in which order, on a project.[10]

So, where should a smart organization go to find an up-and-coming efficiency expert? I would recommend they go down to a local church and ask for the woman everyone looks to for putting a big dinner event together. Or go to the elementary school and talk to the principal about the chairman of the homeroom mothers. That is where you will find an efficiency expert who knows better than to waste either time or money. I would wager she has developed the arranger skill to a high level.

Mediating

Some of the most skillful and effective conflict resolvers I have known are women who learned the art by daily helping six- and eight-year-olds work out who was going to get to play with the Etch A Sketch next. I know a mother of six who I'm convinced could solve the Arab-Israeli conflict if we could find a way to turn her loose in the Middle East.

> So, where should a smart organization go to find an up-and-coming efficiency expert? I would recommend they go down to a local church and ask for the woman everyone looks to for putting a big dinner event together.

Women who have developed the skill of mediation have the amazing ability to maintain their perspective and objectivity in emotionally charged situations. Again, women's emotional intelligence and natural empathy make them especially powerful in this role.

Mediation is a potent skill in the hands of a leader.

During my tenure at the Tennessee Film, Entertainment & Music Commission, I learned the lessons of how essential mediation is to solid business processes. I also came to realize how valued the skill is by all participants in the process. Many supposed impasses between labor and production were resolved by having everyone sit together at a table, work through their differences, and come to an understanding. Such an outcome is much more likely when you have someone in the mix with practical experience at mediation.

Optimizing

This skill is not the same as the making-over skill I described earlier. Making over is about fixing that which is broken. Optimizing, on the other hand, is the ability to take something good and nudge it over into greatness. Optimizers like to tweak and refine and perfect.

I know a number of women who have developed this skill, and it is impressive to see it in operation.

Susan, for example, took over the chairmanship of an annual decorators' show home event that had been held in her city as a charity fund-raiser for more than twenty years. The outgoing chairman had held the position since the event's inception and had built it into a major fund-raising success with lots of momentum and tradition behind it.

Susan knew this. She also knew that very little about the event had changed in more than a decade. As an optimizer, however, she knew better than to try to remake the event in her own image. She wasn't about to try to fix what wasn't broken. But she did see some ways to make the event even more effective, more efficient, and more excellent.

She implemented a small change in the way tickets to the show home were distributed that increased the net receipts to the bottom line by 10 percent. She instituted a media preview day that resulted in increased exposure for the project, which in turn led to higher ticket sales and greater public awareness of the cause for which they were raising money. And she opened up the printed programs to selected advertisers, using some of the additional revenue generated to upgrade all of the promotional materials used in the event.

She simply took something that existed and tweaked it to make it better. Where did Susan develop this skill? Primarily from stepping in to help with her father's business when he started battling a chronic illness.

Creating/Visioneering

Creativity, imagination, and strategic vision are not skills per se; they are gifts—more along the lines of the strengths we explored in chapter 5. And yet there are people who have learned to apply those strengths to the task at hand. They know how to put creativity and vision to work, and that *is* a skill.

It's fun to be in the presence of a strong creative thinker who has just had a fresh challenge thrown in her lap. She will take that problem and turn it over in her mind, examining it from every side. She will explore out-of-the-box approaches, and invariably an innovative solution will emerge.

In a similar way, I have known women who have learned to *see* where an organization can go, what it can become, and how that future can come to pass. I cannot think of a better example than Nancy Brinker.

As her sister lay dying in 1980, Nancy made a solemn promise to do everything she could to end the scourge of breast cancer for all time and for all women. Out of that promise came a vision for a 5K race to raise research funds and awareness. And from that vision the Susan G. Komen foundation was born. Today, Komen for the Cure is the world's largest grassroots network of breast cancer survivors; the Race for the Cure is the world's largest 5K race series; and more than $1 billion has been raised and invested in pursuit of the fulfillment of that promise.

There really is no limit to what a woman with vision can accomplish.

Everywhere I go in this country I find women who are similarly gifted with vision, hope, and creativity. They have spent years building their visioneering muscles on small, unsung projects in unknown places and now wield the strength to envision great things.

Time to Take Inventory

The preceding pages describe fourteen skill types. This is by no means a complete or comprehensive list, but it does contain many of the most common—and commonly overlooked—skills that women develop to meet the demands of daily life as homemakers, moms, wives, volunteers, and employees.

Now it is time to evaluate your own journey and experiences up to this point with an eye toward identifying the transferable, marketable skills you have acquired along the way.

On the following pages you will find a work sheet on which you can begin this process. (You will find even more comprehensive help and assessment tools on the Web site companion to this book: www.yourlifeequity.com.) It's time to give yourself credit for life experience!

Life Experience

In the left column, write down the various roles, jobs, and duties you have performed in your life up to this point. Include personal family roles such as wife and mother, nonpaid roles such as student and Sunday school teacher, as well as traditional professional and work roles such as bookkeeper and sales representative. In the right column, write down any of the skill types that you acquired in that role. Pick from those listed on the preceding pages (Organizing, Multitasking, Rallying, Executing / Facilitating, Negotiating, Crisis Managing, Making Over, Networking / Connecting, Promoting, Mentoring / Coaching, Arranging, Mediating, Optimizing, Creating / Visioneering) or add your own skill type descriptions.

Life Role   Skill Types Acquired

1. _____   _____

                            _____

                            _____

2. _____   _____

                            _____

                            _____

3. _____   _____

                            _____

                            _____

4. _____   _____
   _____
   _____

5. _____   _____
   _____
   _____

6. _____   _____
   _____
   _____

7. _____   _____
   _____
   _____

8. _____   _____
   _____
   _____

9. _____   _____
   _____
   _____

10. _____   _____
   _____
   _____

Putting It All Together

Strengths + Passions + Experience = Life Equity

You have taken the first steps in recognizing and celebrating the skills with which your life experience has equipped you.

In chapter 5, we saw that the "strengths" part of the equation can be viewed through a number of different popular approaches, including the Clifton/Gallup StrengthsFinder® model and the Holland Vocational Personality Types model, or by simply describing your strengths in your own terms.

In chapter 6, we explored the role of passions and interests and the reasons it is so important to have a clear and accurate view of what your true passions are.

As you synthesize these three elements, a compelling picture should emerge of all you bring to the leadership table. Put in different terms, these three factors could be described as your "leanings," your "loves," and your "life lessons." In other words, your life equity. This unified picture should also offer you some direction about where you should be looking to apply that equity—that is, what kind of leadership opportunities you should be seeking.

Your unique equation could be written out in the form of a narrative or synopsis. The template below will give you a start, but you will probably want to expand and adapt it on another sheet of paper.

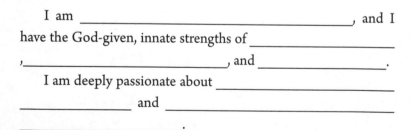

I am _____, and I have the God-given, innate strengths of _____ ,_____, and _____.
    I am deeply passionate about _____ _____ and _____ _____.

And my rich life experiences have endowed me with the following marketable, sought-after skills: _____,
_____, _____,
and _____.

It Is Time to Step Out and Step Up

Our times are crying out for a new approach to leadership—one at which women excel and are uniquely equipped to deliver. And you know in your heart that there is more in you than the world has yet seen. You may not have thought of yourself as a leader in the past—or even as a person who should desire to be one. But you long to make a difference, to have a bigger impact, to cut a wider swath through life.

In the chapters that follow, I want to share with you some things I have learned that can help you make that difference . . . have that impact . . . cut that wide swath. In the process, my hope is that you'll hear and accept the call to leadership and embrace the role of leader.

Life Equity Profile #7

ANNIE WILLIAMSON

Homegrown Efficiency

Annie Williamson's hands trembled a little as she walked over to the big table to complete the two-hour test. She hoped no one noticed how nervous she was. Although she had been practicing her typing skills recently, she now realized no typing was involved in the testing that day. She glanced around at the scores of other women overflowing the large room and tried to imagine *their* situations. Surely no one needed this job as much as she did. Annie pulled out the heavy chair and sat down. She discovered that the test consisted of math, English, and vocabulary questions.

The years of the Great Depression had been especially tough on large, working-class families around Annie's Mobile, Alabama, home. The onset of World War II, though demanding sacrifice and austerity from everyone, had at least created a welcome boom in industry and employment in the area. But that boom proved to be temporary. In the years following the war, the economic fortunes of the Alabama coast slid back to near-Depression-era levels.

Annie had seen all three of these phases in her short life. She had been the middle child of seven as her farmer father did his best to provide for his family in the dark days of the Depression. Her central position in the family and the deprivations of the times combined to produce a girl who was resourceful, hard working, adaptable, and, most of all, curious. In fact, her father had always said that if he needed a particularly difficult job done, Annie was the one he would call upon. When it came to schoolwork, her diligence kept her working by oil lamp late into the night, until every math problem was complete and correct.

Now, in the postwar period, Annie found herself with seven children of her own—ranging from a junior in high school down to three-year-old twins. Her husband was doing the best he could in a blue-collar job, but month after month there simply was not enough money to meet the family's needs, nor was there any form of medical insurance for her or her children. This had brought Annie to the difficult decision to seek a job opening she had heard about at the nearby U.S. Air Force supply depot.

Annie fought a rising tide of discouragement as she drove home from the interview. Upon first arriving at the depot, she found she was one of more than two hundred and fifty women applying for that single job opening. Times were that hard. Jobs were that scarce. It was a long shot, and she knew it.

She turned down her driveway and was greeted by her oldest girls who motioned for her to roll down the window. "How was it, Mother? Did you get the job, Mother? Was the test hard? Oh, tell us about it!"

"Now, girls, there were a lot of other women there," Annie answered. "They probably need that job just as much as we do. We'll just have to see what the good Lord will do."

They escorted the car into the little carport as if it were a royal coach, and when Annie climbed out, the girls surrounded her with a collective hug. "You're so brave," they said. Annie smiled. She felt herself to be many things at that moment, but *brave* was not among them.

The next day the phone rang. She had the second-highest score on the test. They wanted her to come in for an interview.

As Annie entered the office for her meeting, she noticed a well-dressed, attractive woman waiting. *That must be the woman who scored higher*, Annie thought, suddenly feeling self-conscious about her hand-sewn dress. *She looks like she already has a job.*

"Annie Williamson?" the receptionist called out. "He's ready to see you now."

Annie's heart raced as she rose to her feet. "Lord, you know how much I need this," she prayed as she walked through the open door. "Please help me say something right."

She recalled that her father had always advised her to "look them in the eye and tell the truth."

The truth was, her skills were limited, but she was willing and able to learn anything. The truth was, the closest thing to an official position she had ever held was teaching Sunday school for many years. That, in her view, had given her valuable experience in relating to people. It was also true that as the mother of seven children she might not always be available to work if one of them was sick. They would come first. Finally, it was true that she needed the job desperately.

So that is precisely what she told him.

"The phone is ringing!" one of the kids yelled from down the hall the following day. Annie steeled herself and picked up the receiver. It was the gentleman who had interviewed her. He was calling to inform her that he had given the job to someone else.

"However," he said, "I have not been able to sleep since I interviewed you. I was so impressed with your honesty about your situation that I went to personnel and asked them for an additional position, just so I could hire you. How much time do you think you will actually have to take off because of your children?"

"I don't know, but I will be there every day I possibly can," she answered.

Annie hung up the phone and daydreamed about the groceries and school shoes the little bit of extra income would enable her to buy. She scooped up one of the three-year-olds at her feet and headed to the front room to share the good news with the rest of the family!

The following week, the old sedan sputtered out of the driveway and down the street toward the nursery school and her new adventure. Annie looked in the rearview mirror at her still-sleeping twins clutching their blankets on the back seat. A wave of guilt and anxiety swept over her. Maybe the women at church were right. Maybe she shouldn't be leaving her kids to go to work. "How in the world do you think you can work full-time and do justice to those children?" they had challenged. Annie pushed those thoughts aside. *After all,* she thought, *I am only going to do this for a year or two . . . until we get back on our feet.*

From the very first day, Annie took her work seriously. Her natural curiosity drew her to learn everything she could about the processes of which she was now a part. She didn't just want to know *what* to do. She wanted to know *why* it was done that way.

"You're asking questions that nobody else in this job has ever asked," her boss told her one day as they were working on a project.

"Well, I just hate to even handle this stuff without knowing what it is and where it is going," she replied. Soon Annie realized this was not just about working a couple of years for some grocery money. This was a truly interesting place to work.

Each year when the annual performance ratings were given, Annie received a high assessment. One year a young air force lieutenant, who was an industrial engineer, was sent to her office with the objective to improve production. He studied each person's method of accomplishing the same workload. He reported that Annie's work area was best arranged and the workload accomplished most efficiently. When asked where she had learned that, she told him that as an economy measure she had always sewed clothes for herself and her five daughters and had always cooked meals from scratch. This, added to the everyday task of taking care of her family, had taught her to prioritize and make every minute of every day (and sometimes night) count.

At the same time, there was the small matter of seven children at home. Although her older daughters were learning to cook, there was still a lot of work waiting for her at the end of each long day. "You make the best biscuits, Mother!" her kids would say. This was motivation enough. Her love and devotion for them kept her fueled as she continued to cook and sew. Annie's lamp burned well into the night.

Although her responsibilities both at home and at the office grew, Annie was enjoying her life. Working for the air force had broadened her view of the world and bolstered her confidence. Furthermore, her numerous contributions to the efficiency and effectiveness of the operation got her noticed by her superiors—earning her promotions to ever-higher positions. In fact, Annie eventually climbed about as high as a woman could go without a degree or being an active duty officer. In civil service parlance, she had moved from being a Level Two to a Level Seven and was supervising a staff.

This pivotal point in Annie's journey came just as the first computers began to be deployed in major corporations and for government use. Thus it came as no surprise that the Air Force Logistics Command under which Annie worked decided to begin the process of computerizing the global distribution system for parts and supplies. In fact, the supply depot in Mobile was selected to be the location for development and implementation of the new system.

Before long the air force sent a team of mainframe computer specialists to Annie's department to begin the transfer of data from old-fashioned paper to space-age computer tape. Because Annie was so familiar with the existing system and data, she was often called in on the weekends to expedite this process and provide insights. She worked alongside these world-class experts as they wrote the manuals that would ultimately be used as a roadmap for other depots around the nation and the world.

"Annie, I don't know what we would do without your help on this," one of the specialists told her.

She couldn't help but laugh to herself. It was hard to believe that she was the same person who had walked in the door not seven years earlier, wondering if she was going to be able to type well enough to land a low-paying job! But there were more surprises to come.

One day not long after, she heard, "Annie, I need to see you in my office." It was her boss.

"Annie, I have some exciting news!" he said. "The head of the air force computer task force has personally requested that you fill out an application to transfer to the Air Force Logistics Command in Dayton, Ohio. They are implementing the same new system in all other U.S. Air Force Supply Depots, and they want you on the project. It means a promotion for you if you take the job, and there will be more to come. I hate to lose you, but I think it would be a great opportunity for you. Think about it."

Think about it she did. At first blush, it seemed exciting, but she wasn't sure if it was really possible. She would have to leave three of her older daughters behind, not to mention several generations of extended family.

"I just don't know if this is the right thing to do!" Annie told her husband later that night.

"Of course it's the right thing to do, Annie!" he replied. "This is an amazing opportunity. And I can get work anywhere. I think you should take it."

By Friday, Annie's application was on its way to Air Force Logistics Command in Dayton. By Monday morning, they had called to tell her she had the job. They had only one question: "How soon can you come?"

With much trepidation, Annie and her family began the 830-mile trip to their new life in Dayton. Although there were fears about new schools, new friends, new coworkers, her husband's work, and leaving all the young adult children behind, Annie knew that a kind, providential hand had opened this door.

For the next eighteen years, Annie applied her unique skills and talents at the Logistics Command Center at Wright-Patterson Air Force Base—one of the busiest and most important in the world. She became a valued leader and manager in her department as a computer analyst. Just as she had done in Mobile, she applied the eye for efficiency, organization, and systems she had developed by necessity as a child in—and later mother of—a large family with minimal resources.

She taught others how to use the systems she had helped create. Her accomplishments had far superseded anything she could have ever dreamed of. She had traveled to places she never imagined she would go and done things she never dreamed she would have the opportunity to do. In fact, an official air force

Web site says Wright-Patterson has "evolved into the head-quarters for the Air Force's worldwide logistics system and all Air Force systems development and procurement."[1]

Annie tried to retire at age sixty, moving with her husband back to her native Alabama and closer to grandchildren. But after a few quiet years, she received another phone call from the air force.

"Annie, our computer systems contractor wants you to work for them as an advisor and consultant. They're very motivated. They'll pay you nicely and take care of all your expenses. You can even commute from Mobile."

Annie decided she was up for one more challenge. For the next several years she traveled to Ohio on Mondays and home to her husband and family on Fridays, every two weeks. Then she retired for good.

Across three decades Annie Williamson blazed trails of opportunities at a time in which women with large families and limited education simply didn't do such things. By combining keen intelligence with gumption and raw determination, she met her family's needs and, in the process, built a rewarding and fulfilling life for herself.

Now a vigorous eighty-six, she looks back on a professional life she would have never dreamed possible back in sterner, leaner times when nervous hands hit typewriter keys in the desperate hope for a little grocery money and school shoes.

CHAPTER 8

Embracing a Feminine Model of Leadership

> Great necessities call forth great leaders.
>
> —ABIGAIL ADAMS

Moses, Alexander the Great, Marcus Aurelius, George Washington, Abraham Lincoln, Winston Churchill, Mahatma Gandhi, Martin Luther King Jr., Ronald Reagan. When the subject is "great leaders," we have forty centuries of history conditioning us to think of *men*.

As I stated in the opening pages of this book, for most people, we women included, the word *leader* carries masculine connotations. But that is changing. Just look at Sarah Palin. I believe this trend is a very good thing. I don't say that because I think we need female leaders *instead* of male ones. I am contending that we need women to rise up and take places of leadership *alongside* men.

I am definitely not of the "men are pigs" school of feminism. If you are looking for a screechy, bitter diatribe on why the world would be a better place if all men disappeared tomorrow, you'll have to look elsewhere. I think men are great (especially that hand-some guy I married). And there is much about men and masculinity that I admire and value.

But as I pointed out in the opening of this book, there is an emerging awareness of a powerful and effective style of leadership centered very much on openness, trust, teamwork, relationships, and empathy—attributes that are core strengths for many women. Most organizations and businesses will greatly benefit from such leadership. And frankly, I believe the challenges we face as a cul-ture demand it.

For example, a study at Cornell University's Johnson Graduate School of Management found that "compassion and teamwork building will be two of the most important characteristics busi-ness leaders will need for success a decade from now."[1] Of course, countless studies have also shown what most of us know intuitively and through observation, namely, that empathy and teamwork are feminine specialties.

What liberating and exhilarating news it is to learn that we can be dynamic, effective leaders and remain feminine in every way—that, in fact, the very attributes that are the core of femininity are actually strengths in this style of leadership!

Before I share some of what I have discovered to be the keys to developing as a leader, let's take a closer look at this girl-friendly approach to leadership and why it is so important.

You've Come a Long Way, Baby

The American workplace, like the American cultural land-scape, has undergone enormous transformation during the last fifty years. In 1958, only 34 percent of adult women worked outside the home, and those who did tended to work at the lowest levels of the corporate hierarchy. How much things have changed!

Today, by some estimates, 78 percent of women with school-age children work at least part-time outside the home.[2] And we're not stenographers and typists anymore. We're managers, vice presidents, COOs, CFOs, CEOs, owners, and consultants.

Meanwhile, there is an explosion of entrepreneurship going on among women. Women-owned businesses have been starting up at about double the rate of other businesses.[3] During a recent five-year period, women were starting new businesses at a rate of 424 per day, 365 days a year.[4]

This means that vast numbers of women are faced with the challenges of leading a staff in pursuit of their respective visions. From my work on Capitol Hill, I know that small business and entrepreneurship are the twin engines of our nation's economy. Thus, in a very real sense, our nation's economic fortunes are tied to the success of women-owned businesses. And the success of those businesses is tied to their owners' skills as leaders. That is one reason I am so passionate about this subject.

> In a very real sense, our nation's economic fortunes are tied to the success of women-owned businesses.

Why Women Can Make Great Leaders

In 1958, men comprised the large majority of persons involved in business, government, and civic affairs. And the majority of those men had served in the military. That meant that a single approach to leadership would suffice—and that single approach was a top-down, command-and-control style familiar to soldiers and football players. This George Patton / Knute Rockne style of leadership emphasized individualism, self-sufficiency, and competition.

The values and strategies of organizations are increasingly centered on relationships—the very area in which women tend to shine.

But we're in a new age now. Today half of the people involved in the various realms of work and life are women. And the men who make up the other half are a much less homogenous group than they were fifty years ago.

We are living in a time in which the style of leadership best suited for many organizations is one that emphasizes team building and group success over individual accomplishment—collaboration over competition. The values and strategies of organizations are increasingly centered on relationships—the very area in which women tend to shine.

This means that women may actually have a built-in leadership advantage in many situations. This is precisely the case Joanna Krotz, a columnist for Microsoft's online Small Business Center, made when she outlined the following "female leadership strengths." According to Krotz:

- Women tend to be better than men at empowering staff.
- Women encourage openness and are more accessible.
- Women leaders respond more quickly to calls for assistance.

- Women are more tolerant of differences, so they're more skilled at managing diversity.
- Women identify problems more quickly and more accurately.
- Women are better at defining job expectations and providing feedback.[5]

Some in the field of leadership studies have labeled this approach as "soft leadership skills" in contrast to traditional "hard" management skills built around pure performance numbers, incentives, individual rewards, and fear. As one management consultant describes it:

In managerspeak, the word "hard" means good or important. There are "hard results" and "hard numbers," which are better than soft results and soft numbers. And there are "hard skills" which often seem to be much more highly rated than "soft skills."

Now we get a study from the Center for Creative Leadership. It tells us that in tough times, those soft skills are really important. But, guess what, they're not only important in tough times and they're probably more important than those hard skills just about any time.[6]

More and more, organizations are coming to value leaders who get results through a focus on collaboration, communication (particularly the *listening* side of the exchange), and caring. With each passing week, awareness grows that a high EQ (emotional intelligence quotient) is every bit as important in a leader as IQ. People near me are accustomed to hearing me recite the truism:

"In order to move people to where they need to be, you must first meet them where they are."

Remember that valuing relationships is not the opposite of valuing results. Slowing a process so that a team member can get up to speed or become part of the plan will many times *increase* the likelihood of a successful result. Listen. Show sympathy. Then move toward a definition of the problem and your proposed solution.

Certainly there are men who operate in this mode at a high level, and we all know some women who don't. But generally, women are well positioned to excel in this form of leadership.

That doesn't mean, however, that any woman can be a successful leader simply because she is compassionate and willing to listen. Far from it. Leadership is a skill. It is a craft characterized by specialized knowledge, principles, and practices that great leaders learn, follow, and do. On the pages that follow, we will explore these truths and see them in action.

Two Key Ingredients

I have been a student of leaders and leadership for some time now, and I have observed something significant. I have noticed that whenever an individual—male or female—is successful in leading a group of people to greatness, there are two key elements evident in the dynamic of the relationship. Those elements are trust and core values.

It is trust—built upon and earned by consistently displayed integrity—that enables a leader to move an organization in a positive direction. It is trust that will allow a group to know that the leader has its best interest at heart. And whether it is a corporation, a volunteer organization, or a family, trust and confidence in the leader is essential.

Think about it. Have you ever seen it work any other way? Have you seen positive growth in any entity that did not have the underpinning of trust?

I came across a poignant reminder of the power of trust in a story shared by Linda Abraham on the weblog[7] she maintains in support of her business, Accepted.com—a consultancy for people seeking admission to elite graduate schools. Linda lost a young son to leukemia in 1997. On the eighth anniversary of her son's passing, she recalled a powerful lesson in leadership that came from the mouth of her ailing six-year-old.

She described how Joshua had been "a typical, needle-phobic little boy" before being diagnosed with leukemia and how concerned she had been upon hearing that his treatment was going to involve a regular series of painful spinal taps requiring the insertion of a needle into his back. How would a little guy who ran the other direction at the mere mention of a shot sit still for such a procedure over and over again?

Driving home after the first of these spinal taps, Linda wanted to praise and affirm Joshua for getting through it. She wrote in her blog:

> "Joshua, you did a great job!" I told him.
>
> Just six years old then, he had marched into the treatment room, climbed up onto the table, curled into a ball, and with [nurses] Fran's and Maria's encouragement, held still without apparent difficulty. I was impressed. No, I was amazed.
>
> He quietly accepted my accolades, but as we got off

the freeway he shared the credit. "Mommy, when you're with good people, it is easier to be good. And we're with *really* good people."

I almost drove off the road when he said that.[8]

Linda wondered what these nurses had done to inspire such trust in a frightened, frail little boy. On their next visit, Linda asked Nurse Maria that very question. Maria's answer was: "I explained 'Our Rule' about telling kids the truth and always telling them when they would be having something uncomfortable done."

As Nurse Maria would later recall, in the months to come, Joshua helped to enforce this rule more than any other child she had met: "If you wanted Joshua's trust and cooperation, you had to keep your end of the bargain first. Once that trust was established, he was able to cope with even the most painful procedures."[9]

> "When you're with good people, it is easier to be good."

What an extraordinary demonstration of the power of trust to move people to endure, to sacrifice, to persevere under tough circumstances. This wise caregiver knew that trust and cooperation could only grow in an atmosphere of complete honesty and transparency. It is a lesson that was not lost on Joshua's mom.

"Trust is a critical element in leadership," Linda wrote. "Leadership is not about grandstanding or being a loud-mouth or being 'cool.' It's about consistency, reliability, and trust. . . . Integrity is key to leadership."[10]

How saddened I am to note that Joshua lost his battle with cancer after a seventeen-month fight. But how I admire the way his courageous mom, Linda Abraham, has taken a vivid lesson in the power of trust and now applies it to help her clients be more effective leaders. As Joshua understood, "When you're with good people, it is easier to be good."

Trust blooms in an atmosphere of integrity.

The second key element you will always find in the presence of effective leadership is a set of *clearly defined and shared core values.*

The greatest leaders articulate their passions and priorities clearly and consistently. This is what leadership consultant Bob Boylan calls "deciding what's important around here."[11] It refers to a leader's need to establish and hold up those things that she holds sacred. Boylan describes it:

> These basic values, the answer to the question, "What's important around here?" form the platform from which all leaders operate. They are the foundation on which all direction and plans are built. They are the underlying principles that *will* be lived up to, or you cannot survive in the organization.[12]

In this process of articulating her core values, a leader will see two things happen. She will attract those who share those values, *and* she will impart those values to others as they "catch her vision" and heart. Vision is infectious!

For example, if a leader says (and shows) that honesty, justice, loyalty, and charity are highly valued and prominent in her core being, then people she leads will come to share those values, or they won't hang around very long. Such a leader will enjoy a great deal of loyalty and commitment because—as we saw in the example of Joshua—those she leads will operate from a base of trust, knowing she has their best interests at heart.

Any leader—whether she is running a civic club, a county, or a country—will enjoy greater prospects for success if she has cultivated these twin elements of trust and shared values.

Articulating your core values clearly and compellingly requires knowing precisely what they are. As with the passions and interests we explored in chapter 5, you would be surprised at the number of aspiring leaders who haven't taken the necessary time of introspection and self-evaluation required to really understand what is most important to them.

To hear some people talk, *everything* is vitally important to them. For example, a business owner may claim to simultaneously hold profit *and* growth *and* quality *and* market share *and* stability *and* risk avoidance as core business values. But it is simply not possible to do so.

Nor is it possible on a personal level to hold integrity, relational harmony, adventure, and security all at an equally high level. Sometimes acting with integrity violates relational harmony. Preserving harmony means fudging on integrity. Some things must trump other things. One can't always be both adventurous *and* secure. A choice will be made, and it is the most closely held value that will drive that choice.

> One can't always be both adventurous *and* secure. A choice will be made, and it is the most closely held value that will drive that choice.

Often I see a gap or disconnect between a person's *stated* values and his or her *demonstrated* values. Again, a business owner's stated value may be "customer service," while his *demonstrated* value is "beating the competition on price." Our real values are displayed in our choices.

I cannot tell you what your core values are or what they ought to be. These things you must determine for yourself. But I can tell you that a set of values that inspires and energizes others, along with an approach that engenders trust in them, are two elements common to all who lead successfully.

Your mother may have been like mine and reminded you that actions speak louder than words. That is a great summation of this point. The actions of your organization must be consistent with your mission. If your team is to believe in you, your instructions to them must line up with the actions you model before them.

Inconsistency violates trust.

The Perfume of the Flower

Some of the side benefits of serving in Congress are the many opportunities I have to speak to women, young and old. Frequently my subject is leadership, but no matter what my topic, one of the things I invariably try to touch on is the power of formulating a clear, coherent philosophy of life and, within that, a resonant political philosophy.

On one occasion after a speech, a woman thanked me for using the term *philosophy of life*. As she struggled to find her footing in a new stage of life, she had recently pondered the age-old question, is this all there is? She had never thought she was significant enough to need to develop a personal philosophy or mission statement and write it out. She had a self-described "I'm just a cog in the wheel" mentality.

Engaging in the important exercise of formulating a clear philosophy of life involves the ability not just to declare what you believe but also make a case for *why* you believe it. I love what the early twentieth-century journalist George Matthew Adams wrote about this very thing:

> Every one of us, unconsciously, works out a personal philosophy of life, by which we are guided, inspired, and corrected as time goes on. It is this philosophy by which we measure out our days, and by which we advertise to all about us the man, or woman, that we are. . . . It takes but a brief time to scent the life philosophy of anyone. It is defined in the conversation, in the look of the eye, and in the general mien of the person. It has no hiding place. It's like the perfume in the flower—unseen, but known almost instantly. It is the possession of the successful and the happy.[13]

A coherent philosophy of life will very likely incorporate your religious beliefs—including your assumptions about the nature of mankind and our responsibilities as individuals. It will also extend to the political sphere even if you don't pursue an active role in politics. A more current word for such a philosophy of life would be *worldview*. And though everyone has one, not every worldview is well-defined, well-founded, or very well thought out.

The latter must *not* be the case for women who aspire to leadership and influence. If you want to make a difference, you have to know in your heart of hearts what kind of difference it is you want to make. And it is hard to inspire anyone to follow when you're not sure where you're going or why the trip is worthwhile.

That is why I encourage all women to read and evaluate a variety of viewpoints, to keep an open mind, and to ultimately come to a solid understanding of what is true and what is important.

Personally, I was drawn to the political process and community volunteerism—not only because service to country in the cause of preserving our freedom was so vividly modeled in previous generations of my family, but also because I am a wife, a mother, and a businesswoman. In those roles I learned early on that economic freedom and political freedom are inseparable. I also had a strong desire to make my community a better place to live—for my children and for their children yet unborn.

My values, my experiences, and my reading came together to form a solid worldview and a set of unshakable beliefs. Out of these grew a personal mission statement that has illuminated my goals and informed my choices.

I strongly recommend you develop your own personal mission statement. It can serve as a light in dark places, as a compass when you're not sure of your direction, and as a filter when you need to sort out your priorities. Apply your pen to a clean sheet of paper and write out what is important to you and why. It can be simple and to the point or complex and multifaceted. Walt Disney's personal mission statement was simply "To make people happy."

And though the term *mission statement* hadn't been coined when she wrote these words more than one hundred years ago, the poet Bessie Stanley essentially articulated her personal mission statement and her philosophy of life when she penned:

To laugh much; to win respect of intelligent persons and the affections of children; to earn the approbation of honest critics and endure the betrayal of false friends; to appreciate beauty; to find the best in others; to give one's self; to leave the world a little better, whether by a healthy child, a garden patch, or a redeemed social condition; to have played and laughed with enthusiasm, and sung with exultation; to know even one life has breathed easier because you have lived—this is to have succeeded.[14]

The final line of that statement points up a key benefit of creating a meaningful mission statement—it defines success. Many people don't know whether they are succeeding or not because they have no clear inner picture of what success looks like! (At yourlifeequity.com, the companion Web site to this book, you will find a tool that can assist you in forging a meaningful personal mission statement.)

Good News

My hope is that in everything I have presented up to this point you have found two overarching good news themes.

> The preeminent style of leadership that is emerging in the twenty-first century plays directly to the strengths of most women. We are positioned to lead!

Good News Theme #1: Everything you have done up to this point in your life is valid preparation for higher and bigger things. Greater influence, a bigger positive impact, and opportunities to achieve something wonderful and make a difference are possible. In other words, real leadership is available to you.

Good News Theme #2: Leadership doesn't have to look and feel masculine. In fact, the preeminent style of leadership that is emerging in the twenty-first century plays directly to the strengths of most women. We are positioned to lead!

That influence will only be realized—that positive impact will only happen—if we proactively take steps to become those leaders that are so urgently needed in the days to come. There are some habits, principles, and practices commonly followed by people who successfully mobilize others in a worthy cause or important endeavor. Women who know them and practice them will have an advantage going forward. That's where we're headed.

Life Equity Profile #8

JULIE NOVAK

A Dramatic Development

Elite, fifty-year-old private schools simply don't hire teachers who don't have at least one college degree—especially when that school is in the heart of California's Silicon Valley, the epicenter of American technology and innovation. And they certainly don't hire faculty teachers without degrees or certification. It simply doesn't happen.

But it just had.

Julie Novak placed the cordless phone back in the charger and exhaled for the first time in several seconds. She still wasn't exactly sure she had heard the caller correctly. She had been fully braced for a polite but firm rejection. Maybe even a blunt, "Are you kidding us?" But instead she had just been welcomed to the Valley Christian Schools faculty as the junior high school's new drama and theater director.

The opportunity represented the fulfillment of a long-held dream, one which had seemed unlikely in the extreme for the thirty-eight-year-old mother of three.

Julie had grown up in Houston, Texas, the daughter of a successful corporate speaker, consultant, and author. She had always been an extremely creative child. Like her father, she loved performing and was constantly re-creating the musical *Mary Poppins* with her friends.

As she entered school, her love for music and the arts grew. Every school project became a play. Every event prompted a musical story. She took every choir class, auditioned for special groups, and gave her first theatrical performance in fifth grade. These early experiences molded who she was, or at least who she wanted to be. At the same time, Julie battled insecurity.

"I didn't always believe in my abilities," Julie remembered. "And my creative nature didn't really lend itself naturally to self-discipline." These two challenges would ultimately jeopardize her dreams of stage and song.

Nevertheless, in high school Julie's entire life evolved around music and drama—and she excelled at both. Then she discovered a new interest. His name was Tim. Tim was a young man who had recently graduated from her high school. While at a party Julie was attending, he had driven by and thrown some trash out the window of his car. Julie picked up the litter and chased the car down the street.

"Hey, buddy!" she said. "When I grow up and have kids, I don't want them living in a polluted world!" She could not see who was in the car, nor did she want to. She walked away and wondered why she had said that. She had never even thought about having children. She did not even know if she wanted to!

Tim was determined to discover the identity of the brash beauty who had given him such a scolding. It required some research, but he eventually learned her name and began to pursue her.

Tim was drawn to Julie's idealistic, artsy personality. She was drawn to his left-brained, rational way of thinking. Barely eighteen—ignoring reality and the advice of her parents—Julie ran off to marry the man of her dreams. She had an idealized view of married life: no one telling her what to do, freedom to sing in a band and stay out all night if she wanted to. She began working in the fashion and entertainment industry, signed with an agent in Dallas, and began what she thought would be the beginning of "happily ever after."

Julie became pregnant in their first year of marriage, and her career-building plans were put on hold as reality set in. "I had been an absolute dreamer up until that point," Julie said. "But I determined that I was going to be good at this parenting thing."

During the next few years, Julie did just that. She became a disciplined young woman. And a good thing it was. Two more babies arrived in a span of three years. She read every book she could find on parenting. She was amazed at how much she loved being a mom and marveled at how frequently her creative gifts could be deployed in parenting.

Julie's house was constantly filled with singing and dancing—every day a living opera. As the children got older, Julie began to teach them to sing and harmonize together. They began performing for churches and joined a children's theater. Julie's church started a community theater group and before long she was acting again. She even began to direct some of the shows, and ultimately the children's playhouse asked her to be a director. The church asked her to direct their benefit shows for the community. Julie was in heaven. She was back in the arts again.

Word began to spread about Julie's gifts. Julie began working part-time at her children's school as the choir director and drama teacher. She was hired to direct their annual productions. Then someone told her about a position that was opening up at one of the largest private schools in the nation. Julie knew it was a long shot, but she typed up a résumé, produced a video of her work . . . and waited.

A flurry of thoughts raced through Julie's mind as she sat outside the office of the superintendent of Valley Christian School, awaiting her interview. None of them was positive. *What could I possibly be thinking? Teaching positions are for teachers,* she mused. *I just need to leave before I pass out from embarrassment!* Just as she had convinced herself to bolt for the exit, the door opened and she was invited in.

The first few minutes of the interview actually went quite well. But just as Julie started thinking she might survive it without a complete humiliation, the superintendent saw something on her résumé and stopped in midsentence. He looked up from her application and asked, "How did you get this far in the interview process with no degree?"

Her heart sank. She swallowed and took a deep breath. "Perhaps it was the extensive history of outstanding successes on my résumé," she responded.

Did I just say that? she thought. *I am now doomed for sure.* He looked down again at her qualifications. There were indeed many: acting classes, workshops, and scores of successful projects.

After what seemed like an eternity, he looked up once more. "If I decide to hire you, our accreditation rules say I cannot hire you as a teacher," he said. "I *could* possibly hire you with the title of theater director and specialist. But I cannot even believe I am considering this." But consider it he did, and Julie got the call a few days later.

Julie spent the next five years building an amazing program for the school—one that attracted many new students. She taught drama classes, show choirs, and ensembles. On many days she had to pinch herself. She could not believe how blessed she had been. Once again her days were filled with drama and singing.

In November 2004, Julie's husband was transferred to Texas. For Julie that meant starting over. She especially dreaded the awkwardness of interviewing for a teaching position without a degree.

However, a team from the school at which she was interviewing had visited her class in California. They had seen her in action and were acquainted with her successes. Furthermore, the school was new. Its leadership knew the school needed to build a successful music and drama program, such as Julie had proven she could build, in order to attract top students and grow.

This time Julie walked confidently into the reception area and announced, "I am here for a two o'clock interview." There were no thoughts of bolting for the door.

CHAPTER 9

The Art and Science of Leadership

> If we don't change, we don't grow. If we don't
> grow, we aren't really living.
>
> —GAIL SHEEHY

B eth is concerned about the "adult"-oriented businesses and clubs that are proliferating in her community. She recently heard that some new ones are planned just blocks away from where her children go to school. She has been talking to other parents, and they share her concern. Everyone seems to be alarmed about the trends and plans, but no one seems to know what to do about it. Beth is considering hosting a coffee at her house to gather concerned parents and discuss solutions.

For some time Carla has hoped to be able to move up to a management position in her company. She enjoys her work and believes in the company's product, but as a single mom she really needs to be earning more. Besides, she knows there is more in her than what is currently demanded by her position. Frankly, she's getting a little bored.

Recently Carla was asked to head up an informal task force to study ways to cut costs and increase efficiency in her division. She rightly views this as an opportunity to show the executives she is management material. This is the opening she has been working and praying for.

––––––––––––

Mindy is a stay-at-home mom and wouldn't have it any other way. With three boys under the age of twelve and a brand-new baby girl, she has her hands full with school, sports, church, Cub Scouts, and more. Her life is a dizzying swirl of activity.

When she manages a few quiet moments to herself, she finds herself worrying about the kids and the world they're growing up in. She and her husband are committed to raising them to be people of character, confidence, and personal responsibility. But the influences of music, television, movies, and the Internet all seem like a giant conspiracy to undermine their influence. She often wonders if she is up to the challenges of shaping their character and giving them a good start.

––––––––––––

Maria had been pondering, planning, dreaming, and scheming about it for much of the last fifteen years. With her youngest about to head off to college, it now seemed the time was right. In fact, it was now or never. She was going to take the leap and launch that little restaurant and catering business.

An ideal spot had opened up among the antique shops and

boutiques on the main street of the cute little historic neighborhood she had been watching for some time. She had scrimped and saved a sizable chunk of start-up capital, although her meticulously crafted business plan showed she would need a small-business loan as well to get her through the first two years and to profitability.

The food, the décor, the advertising, the financials—Maria was confident about all those aspects of her plan. It was the human element that gave her the most pause. As her business plan showed, she needed to hire kitchen staff, wait staff, administrative and sales help, and more.

She was haunted by the knowledge that if she didn't find and keep the right people, her life's savings could be lost—and with it, her life's dream.

These women have dramatically differing objectives and circumstances. They have varying levels of education and divergent backgrounds, and are in different seasons of life. Yet they share one thing. In order to succeed, they each need to function as a leader.

The fact that they have never considered themselves leaders or identified with leadership as an appropriate goal for themselves doesn't matter in the least. Life is *demanding* leadership skills from them. And they will succeed or fail on the basis of their ability to muster them.

The good news for all of them, and hundreds of thousands of other women like them, is that much about leadership can be learned. Indeed, it is part art and part science. As with artistic ability, some people are born with more natural leadership qualities than others. But even the "naturals" must become students of the principles of leadership and put them into practice. As with a science, there are concrete principles and truths that can be learned, applied, and counted on.

And because there are varying styles of leadership, I am convinced that virtually anyone can become an outstanding leader in a style and mode that is right for her.

Leadership Is a Way of Life

Like oxygen in the air, there are some things we just take for granted as long as they are present, but miss acutely when they are not. Leadership can be like oxygen—invisible but vital for organizational life. And when it is not present, the organization begins to die. That is why I tell aspiring leaders: the presence of leadership is not always known, but the absence of leadership is always felt.

Can leadership be invisible? It can indeed. Can leaders fly under the radar? They do it all the time. Leadership rarely involves standing up on a chair with a megaphone or running out ahead of the parade waving one's arms like a majorette. Much of the most effective leadership is quiet. In fact, there is an entire systemized approach to quiet leadership developed by the Hudson Institute called "leading from behind."[1]

This is just one of the numerous leadership styles I mentioned in the previous section. Some women have the temperament, dynamism, and assertiveness to be high-profile leaders. And there are many points on the scale in between the two extremes. Therefore, at the end of the day, leadership is not as it appears but as it performs.

In other words, it doesn't really matter what style the leader adopts or whether it conforms to everyone's preconception about what leadership looks like. What matters is the outcome. What matters are the results. Did the team accomplish its goals? Did we win? There is a growing appreciation for this truth, and that is good news for women. It means we don't have to explain that it is possible to lead without fitting the profile of an NFL quarterback or a four-star general. We're entering the era in which the ability to deliver the results trumps everything else.

> It is possible to lead without fitting the profile of an NFL quarterback or a four-star general. We're entering the era in which the ability to deliver the results trumps everything else.

One thing is certain though: no matter what the chosen style, women who lead successfully do so because they embrace leadership as a lifestyle. You must do the same. The good news is that as a woman, you have a head start!

For example, I believe women instinctively know that you *manage* things but you *lead* people. This is such a vital concept to grasp. It is the difference between merely giving orders to be robotically executed and building a vital, relational working environment. Leadership courses designed primarily for men have to devote a lot of time to helping men adopt that paradigm. As women, our natural empathy, relationship-centeredness, and bias for communication all work together to put us well down the road toward good leadership.

Nevertheless, all truly successful leaders—male *and* female—excel because they learn the fundamental principles of leadership and then weave them through the entire fabric of their lives. The basic tenets are unchanging, but the varying circumstances determine the way in which you apply those principles.

That means there is no shortcut to developing leadership ability. The skills are developed just as muscles are—through the strain and struggle of regular exercise. The more you put into the daily exercise of your leadership skills, the more pliable, more adaptable, and stronger they become.

The following seven core habits will serve you well in your development as a leader.

1. Leaders Commit to Team Building

As I have already noted, women have a built-in advantage on this front. We tend to be much more comfortable speaking in terms of "we" than "me."

I don't like the word *boss*. To me it's a four-letter word carrying loads of negative baggage. Even though I lead a staff of people who work with me both in Washington and back home in my district, I am not the boss of anyone or anything. I do seek to build and lead a team to achieve what I envision to be the goals of the people I represent.

As you build a team, you should seek out people who share your vision and have common values and goals. You should also seek people who desire growth opportunities and who enjoy the challenge of finding ways to expand your vision.

Building a team around you requires that you pull them together as a group to learn, to study, and to build relationships with each other and with you. That is why, when I have chaired organizations, I have preferred to have much of the work done in small groups and committees between the scheduled meetings, and then use the meetings for reporting and final decision making.

When members of a team have the opportunity to learn together, evaluate information, report the findings, and recommend a course of action, the process invariably builds confidence and cohesion among them. Seldom do you find someone who does not respond to being delegated authority to make a decision. When you follow this model, it also requires that those who perform with excellence receive credit for that action.

If team members are not accustomed to accepting responsibility, ease them into the role with simple tasks that can be performed quickly and well. Ask them to assist you or another leader in the group with the implementation of a task. Then ask for their input or evaluation of the task. Follow it with a request for them to take the next step in the process alone.

Realize that there is a role for everyone. Each person needs to know there is a role for him or her within a list of responsibilities. You as the leader need to throw yourself into mentoring them to be sure they attain the goal. Make it your goal to create an environment where success can be fostered, nurtured, and celebrated. They will love you for it. By doing this, you empower others to achieve more, to do better, to surpass you.

Leaders teach what they know and model what they are. That brings us to the next principle.

2. Leaders Raise Up Other Leaders

Mentoring is one of those business buzzwords that is thrown around with increasing regularity these days. Behind the trendy word is a very real principle. It is a principle leadership authority

John Maxwell calls "The Law of Reproduction." Commenting on the adage "Eagles don't flock. You have to find leaders one at a time," Maxwell writes:

> The only way you will be able to develop other leaders is to become a better leader yourself. . . . An environment where leadership is valued and taught becomes an asset to a leadership mentor. It not only attracts "eagles," but it also helps them learn to fly. An eagle environment is one where the leader casts vision, offers incentives, encourages creativity, allows risks, and provides accountability. Do that long enough with enough people and you'll develop a leadership culture where eagles begin to flock.[2]

That's the way it is with leadership. When you go up the ladder, you make a way for others to follow after you. To keep other people down, you have to stay down where they are. Leaders teach what they know and reproduce what they are.

So how do great leaders learn to be effective mentors? In most cases, by having been mentored themselves. Almost certainly, somewhere along the line, they have found someone to counsel, support, and encourage them.

There is no denying it. To be the most effective, successful leader you can be, you have two related tasks: (1) find a mentor and (2) be a mentor.

How important is mentoring to the success of an individual? It is hard to overstate its power.

In her well-researched book about successful women, Donna Brooks, executive vice president of the European Women's Management Development Network cites a study done back in the

'80s of AT&T female managers, which found that women with mentors earned promotions more quickly than those without mentors. Even more telling was the finding that women who were initially evaluated as not having much advancement potential but who had mentors advanced as far or farther than those who were rated as having greater potential but who did not have mentors.[3]

Later in the same book, Brooks writes:

> If I were to choose the most critical success secret, I would have to say that having an effective mentor or advocate is it! When I teach management classes and discuss the changing roles of employees in organizations, I frequently underscore the importance of the mentoring relationship. At the end of the class, as the students are about to leave, I always ask them, "So what's the one thing that I want you to remember, if you remember nothing else from this meeting?" They all chime in, "Get a mentor!"[4]

Allow me to second that advice with an addendum: "Get a mentor and be a mentor!" Do it because "leaders raise up other leaders."

3. Leaders Are Lifelong Learners

Through the years I've had opportunities to speak at many high school and college commencement ceremonies. I'm always honored and happy to do so. One thing I invariably mention, especially to college grads, is that the event is really marking a beginning rather than an end—an introduction rather than a departure. I point out that we are living in an era that increasingly demands we all become, as the popular label puts it, "lifelong learners." I remind them that the statistics indicate they will most likely make seven or eight major career shifts during the course of their lives.

I really am convinced that people who develop the ability to learn—and who take the lead in making learning an ongoing quest—will be at a tremendous advantage in the twenty-first century. Women who make a commitment to daily learning and daily improvement—building on the previous day's progress—will be on the fast track to leader status. This, of course, requires knowing *how* to learn and not being afraid of learning.

I like what the writer Harvey Ullman said: "Anyone who stops learning is old, whether this happens at twenty or eighty. Anyone who keeps on learning not only remains young, but becomes constantly more valuable regardless of physical capacity."

Successful people form the habit of doing things unsuccessful people won't do. Yesterday's success lulls us into today's complacency, which sets the stage for tomorrow's failures.

4. Leaders Are Not Afraid to Fail

Earlier in this book we examined at length the issue of risk aversion in women. We saw that a generally low tolerance for risk commonly coupled with low self-confidence was a major reason many talented, hard-working women didn't reach out and grab opportunities when they presented themselves. I suspect that is why Eleanor Roosevelt advised women: "Do at least one thing every day that scares you."

One of the things that characterizes women who achieve bold goals and bring about big positive changes is the courage to take intelligent risks. In other words, leaders are not afraid to fail. They have learned that failure is not the end of the world—that in fact it is merely a learning opportunity. They have also learned that timidly trying to avoid risk doesn't keep you from having setbacks; it just keeps you from seizing opportunities. In that spirit, management guru Peter Drucker said, "People who don't take risks generally make about two big mistakes a year. People who do take risks generally make about two big mistakes a year."[5]

One morning while reading the *Wall Street Journal*, I noticed an employment advertisement that declared, "We are not looking for people who have never failed. We are looking for people who never give up trying." I liked that, and I've never forgotten it.

The individuals who never give up trying are the ones who are not paralyzed by fear. They take risks and approach new jobs, new technologies, and new adventures in their life as opportunities to grow. They join commitment and perseverance with personal courage to pull away from the pack and make a difference. These are the men and women who push the boundaries, who take action. They are not afraid of failure and will fail many times while passionately pursuing their goals.

Mary Kay Ash had the audacity to think beauty products would sell at home beauty shows. She believed her skin-care products could be sold to small groups of women looking for ways to improve their image and potential for success. Her first home show produced a whopping $1.50 in sales.

Mary Kay had risked her $5,000 in savings on this venture, and $1.50 in sales was not a good return on her investment. She modified her selling techniques, refined the packaging, and adjusted her attitude to succeed. She did $34,000 in retail sales the first year. In 2006, Mary Kay Cosmetics had more than thirty-three thousand independent sales directors spread across the planet

> Leaders know that setbacks are going to come whether they hide in the closet or not, so they might as well come out and give some things a whirl.

producing wholesale sales of $2.25 billion.

Leaders know that setbacks are going to come whether they hide in the closet or not, so they might as well come out and give some things a whirl. They are in search of new opportunities and view challenges in terms of their possibilities for innovation. They know that continuing to work through today's failure gets you closer to the success you hope to see tomorrow.

5. Leaders Consider the Three *R*s of Every Opportunity

I pointed out in chapter 1 that as I began my adult life, I didn't really have any grand strategy or master plan for my life. I knew I wanted to somehow make a positive difference, and I didn't want to be eighty years old and feel I had wasted my opportunities. I simply stepped through open doors as they were presented to me. Or to reverse the metaphor, when key opportunities came knocking, I answered!

That is not to suggest that I have said yes to every offer and opportunity that has come my way. I have learned, in fact, that a key skill is knowing how to evaluate opportunities as they come along. I have discovered that leaders consider the risk, responsibility, and reward of each and every opportunity.

First, let us return to the subject of risk. I have been very clear in my encouragement to become an intelligent risk taker. The operative word in that phrase is *intelligent*. There is nothing admirable about taking risk for risk's sake.

Intelligent risk takers ask, "What are the costs—in terms of time, money, effort, and energy—of saying yes to this opportunity?" Then they do their best to get good answers to that question. Diving into something without having a clear assessment of what it will require from you isn't wise risk taking—it's a blind leap into the unknown. If the cost of saying yes is more than you can pay, it doesn't matter how enticing the reward is. You shouldn't do it.

The second thing to consider when evaluating a new opportunity is the responsibility you will carry. What will you be doing? How much of it can be delegated? Is it something that excites or interests you? Is it consistent with your passion? How does it line up with your personal mission statement? To whom will you be accountable?

Finally, you must assess the upside potential—the reward—and compare it to your assessment of the risk. Is the reward commensurate with the risk? The greater the risk, the greater should be the reward.

If an opportunity makes sense in light of the three *R*s above, by all means go for it—but only if it lines up with your passion and mission. As you move through life, there are many things that may catch your eye, but only a few will catch your heart.

6. Leaders Are Vision Oriented and Principle Driven

Wherever you find a woman exercising leadership, you will find a clear and compelling vision. To lead effectively, you must be vision oriented too.

Your vision doesn't have to be grand or earthshaking. But it does have to be *yours*. It doesn't have to excite millions. But it does have to stir you (and a handful of others). You may have a vision for a better neighborhood, a stronger school system, a business of your own, a promotion, a better job in a new field, or another of a million possibilities. Whatever it is, it must fire you with determination and steel you with resilience.

> It is not enough to possess a vivid and worthy vision. For leadership to take place, others have to catch it. You have to make yourself contagious.

It is not enough to possess a vivid and worthy vision. For leadership to take place, others have to catch it. You have to make yourself contagious. Vision must be shared. Only then can your vision serve as a rallying point for the other members of the team.

The grand, broad brushstrokes of vision must also be translated into the fine lines of tangible, measurable goals. Those goals must be written down and reviewed with the team on a regular basis. Your role as the visionary is to "see" those goals accomplished every day.

Vision compels. It propels. It focuses.

Glenn Van Ekeren, one of the world's most respected leaders in the world of business, said that good leaders "create a vision, articulate the vision, passionately own the vision, and relentlessly drive it to completion."[6]

In the very best of leaders, however, that relentless drive is governed and channeled by something—a force that guides the leader's actions and choices. I'm talking about *principles*. Truly effective leaders aren't just vision oriented; they're principle driven as well.

Principle-driven people recognize that there are laws and standards woven into the very fabric of creation and that we violate those laws at our peril. Such leaders know that certain standards—like always treating people fairly and with respect—aren't *right* simply because they work, but rather that they *work* because they're right.

If faced with a choice between quick success and being faithful to her principles, a leader will remain faithful to her principles. And because of that commitment, she *will* succeed in the long run, with a kind of success that is lasting, sustainable, and not destructive to her soul.

7. Leaders Believe in the Value of Their Own Earned Skills

As a little girl in Sunday school, I learned a story almost everyone knows. It is the Old Testament account of David and Goliath. Who in the Western world isn't aware of the young boy David's boldness and courage in facing the heavily armored, battle-hardened giant—armed only with a sling and a few smooth stones? The story is so widely known in our culture that it has become a metaphor. News reporters will describe an underdog's fight against a more powerful entity as a "David vs. Goliath" situation. What most people forget about that story is the source of David's confidence.

According to the biblical account in 1 Samuel, David was asked why he, a shepherd boy with no combat training, was so confident he could defeat the intimidating champion put forth by the enemy. His reply was telling. He described the challenges he had to overcome in tending his father's sheep. He recounted the times he had to fend off wild animals that threatened the flock. He told the skeptical generals of the Israelite army, "I have defeated the lion and the bear. And I know I can defeat this big-mouthed bully."

In this overlooked aspect of the story is the liberating truth that I have tried to emphasize throughout this book. It is the realization that infused me with confidence when I ran for and won a seat in the United States House of Representatives. And it is the principle we see illustrated so vividly in the stories of the remarkable women it has been my pleasure to share with you in between each chapter. If you take nothing else away from your reading here, please understand and embrace this: Your small, private victories have positioned you for bigger, more public ones. Those things you have learned doing the mundane can be deployed in the majestic. The leadership skills you have honed in one realm of activity will transfer to the next.

You are better, stronger, and more ready than you know.

> Your small, private victories have positioned you for bigger, more public ones. Those things you have learned doing the mundane can be deployed in the majestic.

TAMARA QUINN

A Baghdad Bookaholic in America

Were it not for the fact that she wasn't born in America, Tamara Quinn could give any presidential candidate a run for his or her money on the campaign stump. She speaks of the virtues of life in this country with the appreciation and earnestness that can only flow from one who has tasted oppression and control but who now breathes freely.

"Don't take the American way of life for granted," she warned. "Be vigilant and determined to protect our liberty. Do not think that we are entitled. We must strive to earn our democracy daily." Meaningful words from someone who lived her first nineteen years in Baghdad, Iraq. She escaped the emerging horror of the Baath regime, but at a price— leaving her family and loved ones behind.

Tamara grew up in the Iraq of the 1950s and '60s—before the quasi-Fascist Baath party came to power with the zealous participation of a young Saddam Hussein. Nevertheless, the culture for a young girl there was different than that in America.

"Socially, the life of a girl was very restricted, but educationally and professionally, I was given every encouragement toward the future," Tamara explained. "I had great role models—my mother and my aunt both had master's degrees and were teachers. My father was a doctor, and my uncle was a geologist. Surprisingly, being in Iraq at this time, there was never any question about attaining anything I wanted to do."

Right about the time Tamara was beginning her studies at the University of Baghdad, the situation in Iraq began to change—and not for the better. A revolution brought a Baathist dictatorship into power in 1968, and in the tradition of earlier Nazi and Soviet regimes, the government quickly began to seize control of all the institutions of society, including the universities. It was then Tamara was marked by those she described as "minions of the Baath dictatorship" as a person to keep a close watch on.

The annoying surveillance she endured her freshman year was intensified her sophomore year to include overt harassment. She could see where this all was headed, and it was, in her words, "not very good." So Tamara did something her watchers would never have expected: forfeiting all her hard work and credit for her sophomore year, she slipped out of the country in the middle of the week of her final exams. At nineteen, she arrived alone and unprepared on the shores of the world's promised land—the United States.

"It was a very difficult thing," Tamara said of her escape to America. "My mother and dad were totally against it, and I think it broke my mother's heart. But there was never a question about trusting my own judgment. Looking back on it now, I can't believe I did it. As a young girl in Iraq, you are never left on your own at all. I had very little experience and no idea what to expect."

Amusingly, the primary image of life in the United States that Tamara did arrive with was drawn from the pages of Archie comic books. As a teenager living amidst civil unrest and volatile revolutions every few months, the lives of Archie, Jughead, Betty, and Veronica were a welcome escape. "Archie's life was so uncomplicated compared to the times I was living in. They could just *enjoy* themselves so much," she said.

During these same early years, Tamara's grandfather was intent on making sure that not all of his granddaughter's reading was focused on soda fountain chatter.

"From my earliest memories, I remember my granddad taking me to ancient Al-Mutanabi Street in Baghdad where all the bookstores were. He would have them climb up ladders in different areas of the store to search for books he had chosen for me," Tamara remembered. "One of the first books I read at age eleven was Victor Hugo's *Les Misérables*, translated into Arabic, of course. I think it had a very strong impact on my sense of good and evil."

Other mind-stimulating books such as *The Prophet*, *As a Man Thinketh,* and Ayn Rand's *Atlas Shrugged* soon followed—a pretty heady reading list for a young girl in the Arab Middle East. These challenging works provided "fuel for the fire" of Tamara's love of reading and helped to lay the groundwork for the makings of a self-proclaimed "bookaholic."

"I have always loved books. If there were not ten thousand other good reasons to live in this country, I would be here because of Barnes & Noble!" she said exuberantly.

Tamara finished her college studies at Kentucky's Murray State University with a degree in mathematics; she headed into the world of work, married, and had children— all very much in keeping with one progressively realizing the American Dream. She did discover early on, however, that dream's promise of equality and opportunity is imperfect and not yet fully realized.

"I was denied a promotion at a bank where I was working because I was told those management positions needed to go to men who have to support a family," she said. "Never mind that I had two kids also. I wanted a better life, and I was angry and surprised when I encountered these artificial roadblocks."

She has gone on to earn an additional degree in accounting and launch a long and successful career in the energy industry.

Tamara believes—and her willingness to venture to a strange country to begin a new life attests to it—that her greatest strength may be her "willingness to step into the unknown based on faith in my judgment."

This judgment—what some have called "intuitive wisdom"—has served her well. What she described is not some *feeling* but rather a well-honed ability to remain "totally dispassionate in any kind of situation. To view something for its reality and not be overly affected by emotion. An internal compass, one might say."

Nevertheless, it is both wisdom and emotion that have compelled Tamara to take some extraordinary steps since retiring from the energy industry. The trigger for the first big step came soon after the launch of the Iraq War and the subsequent fall of the Hussein dictatorship in 2003. Tamara was contacted by the Department of Defense and asked to go to Iraq with the Coalition Provisional Authority. She agreed to return to Baghdad and began work with the Iraqi Reconstruction and Development Council (IRDC), a liaison group between the Iraqi leaders and the undersecretary of defense.

After an absence of more than thirty years, this experience kindled in her a desire to stay involved in the historic effort to help her native country and to help bring the American and Iraqi cultures together.

To that end, Tamara has partnered with a number of other Iraqi expatriate women to launch organizations aimed at improving the lives of people in Iraq. The hope of these efforts is that people half a world away might experience some of the same freedoms, opportunities, and blessings this country has afforded her.

For example, Tamara is the founder and executive director of Generation Iraq, an outreach organization dedicated to helping Iraqi youth through educational community-based outreach projects. The program focuses on teaching self-reliance; volunteerism; and helping orphans, the disabled, and young widows realize a better life.

Generation Iraq also sponsors the School Partners Program "to connect schools in the United States with Iraqi schools via the Internet to introduce the young people of the two countries and to allow them to learn that their hopes, dreams, and interests are more similar than they might otherwise realize."

Tamara is also a cofounder of the Women's Alliance for a Democratic Iraq—a group dedicated to "promoting Iraqi women's rights and involved in the ongoing journey to a better and safe Iraq for all Iraqis." One of the group's initiatives is the U.S.-Iraqi Business Sorority Program in which American businesswomen will be paired in a mentoring relationship with Iraqi businesswomen and entrepreneurs. Tamara also serves on the board of directors for the Global Justice Center, and through that group she helped organize and manage two conferences in Iraq and Jordan to train the judges of Iraq in international law and women's rights.

These new ventures in her life have served to use Tamara's management and organizational talents while allowing her to give back to the people of her homeland. "My balance between humanitarian and corporate activity is so good right now," she said, relishing this phase of her life. "It's good for the soul to know that you are doing a good business . . . but trying to help others as well. It's a very good balance, and I'm loving every minute of it."

Tamara Quinn experienced the threat of government oppression as a young person, bravely moved halfway around the world for freedom and a better life, built a successful professional and personal life for herself in her adopted country, and now pursues an astonishing variety of humanitarian and business activities. It is not surprising to learn that one of Tamara's favorite quotes challenges the soul to great deeds: "The greater danger for most of us lies not in setting our aim too high and falling short; but in setting our aim too low, and achieving our mark" (Michelangelo).

Tamara Quinn is aiming high. High aim brought her to America. Now it is taking a little bit of her home again.

CHAPTER 10

What Are You Waiting For?

> When in the world are we going to begin to live as
> if we understand that this is life? This is our time,
> our day . . . and it is passing. What are we waiting
> for?
>
> —RICHARD EVANS

A great American historian observed that there are really two educations: one that teaches us how to make a living; the other, how to live.[1]

We are blessed to live in a country in which, for the overwhelming majority of people, making a living is not the only issue. I believe it is that second education—learning how to truly live—that is the real challenge. I am also convinced the struggle on that count is especially acute for women. Offering some tools to win that battle has been the burden, the vision, and the passion behind this book.

I certainly don't have all the answers, but I have learned that living successfully involves more than merely accumulating wealth, security, status, titles, or accolades. In my view, a life well lived is one in which one's highest potential is applied in pursuit of the greatest good. It is true to self and yet others oriented.

The people I have known whom I consider truly great are the ones who are champions at "living," and who have worked to better their little corners of the world.

As women we are living in a moment in history in which an unbelievable array of options is spread before us. While some vestiges of glass ceilings still exist here and there, the most formidable barriers to our achievement now lie within our own minds and hearts. We're like the elephant that had been chained to a post for years and, though now the chain has been removed, still never ventures more than ten feet from the post.

We have been empowered to choose the role we play in society. If we prefer to stay home and raise a family, we often can. If we aspire to make a mark in the corporate world, we can. Or we can choose some blend of the two, as many do.

Frankly, we are now constrained only by the limits of our courage and imaginations.

My goal in these pages has been to steel your courage and fire your imagination. Why? Because I believe it is our responsibility to accept enlarged roles for ourselves as new doors open; to be fluid in moving from one arena to another, always taking with us the skills we have acquired; to welcome new opportunities as they are presented to us; to acknowledge with grace, rather than embarrassment, our accomplishments and successes; and to serve as guides and champions to those who would follow in our footsteps.

I opened this work by sharing the stories of four real women grappling with four intensely personal questions about their lives, dreams, and futures. I want to close it now by speaking to each of those questions in light of what we have discovered along the way. I hope you will find inspiration and encouragement in the answers.

"Am I Finished?"

This question was the heart cry of stay-at-home-mom Julie, whose last chickadee had recently flown the nest. I have an answer for her: "Heck no, you're not finished. Girl, you're just getting warmed up!"

Julie has twenty-plus years of experience in organizing, promoting, teaching, and mentoring. Barely midway through her forties, she is young (since she lives in an era in which the average lifespan of a woman approaches eighty and is projected to rise dramatically higher). She has talent, energy, intelligence, and now—for the first time in a couple of decades—time. She has everything, in fact, except what she perceives to be a traditional résumé filled with a traditional work history.

I say, "Big deal! Résumés are overrated."

If Julie could see through the present fog of fear and insecurity, she would see that the real question is not, can I find something meaningful to do, but rather, which among the many open paths of adventure and significance should I take? She has options. The world is her oyster, and that world needs her!

A little introspective time filling in the blanks of the life equity equation (Strengths + Passions + Experiences = Life Equity) will help Julie narrow those choices. A fresh overview of her hard-earned life skills in light of her strengths and passions will point her in a general direction. The sum total of those three elements may point her toward a new business venture, a fresh approach to attacking a community problem, or even back to school.

Finished? On the contrary. She's positioned for an exciting new beginning.

"What if I Fall on My Face?"

As you will recall, this was Jamie's paralyzing fear that rose up whenever she considered leaving the security of her corporate job to follow her dream of starting her own new venture.

As we have seen, fear of failure is one of the most common forces keeping women from pursuing their dreams or following their visions for making a difference. And we have learned that those who accomplish big things view the prospect of failure not as the end of the world but as a learning step on the way to success.

To Jamie I would say, "Do your homework. Plan well. Get wise counsel. And if, with your eyes wide open, you still have that itch to launch your venture, then as the saying goes, 'feel the fear and do it anyway.' " I like what entrepreneur and consultant Vickie Milazzo wrote along these lines:

> If you want something better for your life and career, you owe it to yourself to go for it or reject it outright. Don't leave the dream dangling as a reminder of what you don't have the time, courage or enthusiasm to grab. Do it or forget it.
>
> Don't wait for conditions to be perfect. That will never happen. People who wait or dabble usually end up at their retirement party rewarded with a glass of watery

punch and a piece of white cake. Own up to your passions, then step out and grab hold of them with both hands.[2]

"What if I fall on my face?" you ask. Well, then you'll pick yourself up, dust yourself off, and start again. There is no shame in attempting great things. But what a tragedy to miss a chance at doing something truly remarkable simply out of fear of what others might think in the unlikely event that you fail! Go for it.

"Who Will Recognize What I Have to Offer?"

Becky posed this heartbreaking question as she faced a terrifying set of circumstances—in her midfifties, freshly divorced, and in dire need of a decent income. Sadly, it is a situation far too many women find themselves in. Just when they are entering a season of life that should be filled with reward for the decades of sacrifice and putting others first, they find themselves virtually starting over. But you don't have to face a confluence of crises to wonder the same thing.

So who *will* recognize what Becky and others have to offer?

Frankly, lots of people will, *if* these women will cultivate the confidence that comes from believing in the value of their own earned skills. Employers and decision makers are not looking for reasons to disqualify candidates who might be able to play a role in helping them succeed. They are looking for reasons to say yes.

Furthermore, when given a choice between a person with a thin résumé but a confident, can-do attitude and one who looks great on paper but clearly doesn't believe in herself—employers will choose the former nearly every time.

No, not everyone will instantly connect the dots linking your past work as a mom or volunteer leader to the marketable skills those roles instilled in you. That's why you should be prepared to connect those dots for them. Even then, not everyone will get it. Some, like that farmer I encountered on the campaign trail, will remain in the dark. But plenty of folks will get it, and all you need is one yes and you're on your way.

"Do I Have What It Takes to Make a Real Difference?"

Remember Caitlin? She needed to know she was going to leave the world better than she found it. Her question emerged as she wrestled with her inability to be satisfied with a "regular" job. She is not alone. It is a question in the back of the minds of a lot of great women I know. In fact, I spent some time grappling with it myself.

After all, who was I, just a cookie-baking homemaker, to think I could do something to make my country a better place for my children and their children yet unborn? It seemed audacious to me. It still does sometimes.

It is one thing to read about difference makers—to admire their passion and applaud their dedication. It is another thing to contemplate being one of them. They can too easily seem like storybook heroines—larger than life and in possession of powers we mere mortals can't call upon. But from walking the corridors of power in Washington DC and meeting with women leaders around the world, I have learned that they are just like you and me. They struggle with self-doubt, get weary and afraid, and often feel inadequate for the tasks before them.

Such feelings are normal. The determining factor for leadership greatness is not so much ability as *availability*. Michelle Nunn, cofounder of the HandsOn Network, writes:

> We live in a world of self-help, but the most profound and fundamental way to help ourselves lies in our ability to reach out and help others—to extend beyond our own needs to support those around us. . . . Our world is different as a result of countless service leaders. There is a profound truth in Martin Luther King Jr.'s familiar pronouncement that "everybody can be great because everybody can serve." Service is a great equalizer.[3]

During World War II, women rose to the challenge, moving out of the home and onto the factory floor to build tanks, planes, and aircraft carriers—becoming in the process part of what has come to be known as "the greatest generation." I believe that, in a similar way, the challenges of our times are calling us to move into new roles, new zones of influence, and new, sometimes unfamiliar places of responsibility. This call comes just as awareness of a new type of leadership is growing—a leadership style that is ideally suited to play to women's natural strengths.

> The determining factor for leadership greatness is not so much ability as *availability*.

As we rise to confront the threats of our day, we'll form a new "greatest generation."

Do *you* have what it takes to make a difference? I am confident you do. I leave you with a final question—one only you can answer: *What are you waiting for?*

MELINDA SCRUGGS GALE

Record of Success

"I love my life! *I love my life!*" came the confident acclamation from Melinda Scruggs Gales. "Is it perfect? No! Are there things that I wish were different? Of course! Are there things that I constantly work on to be different and change? Absolutely! But thank you very much, I love the ticket I drew," she said as if referring to striking it big on some cosmic lottery pick rather than the hectic, hitting-on-all-cylinders and oftentimes overflowing busy-ness she calls her life these days.

This off-the-charts exuberance for her life is not, as many might assume, the result of a privileged upbringing or even conventional family dynamics. "Just because I love my life doesn't mean that it's been easy," she said in an effort to show that her enthusiasm is hard-fought for, not simply bestowed. "I've had a tough life. I had parents who divorced right before my senior year in high school." And this was the good news.

After a summer of "raging war" amongst her parents resulting in another episode of her father's physical abuse toward her mother, Melinda approached her mom and said simply, "We need to leave. We need to pack up the car and move to Texas." And move they did, to the welcoming arms of extended family in Abilene, Texas. For Melinda, it meant leaving behind the comfort and security of lifelong friends and the anticipation of being a football cheerleader her senior year.

"At that point in my life, the risk was to stay and continue to live in an abusive household, or to take a risk and step out into the unknown for the safety of the family . . . I was sad, but I'm a 'glass half full' person. I thought, *This is going to be a new adventure.*"

A bit of retrospective self-analysis gave way to an explanation of her bravado and maturity at such a young age: "I'm a middle child who acts like the oldest . . . I was blessed with genes that are like 'let's take charge of this situation and figure out a plan and move on it.' But I'm thankful to God that he gave me this kind of genetic makeup . . . Thanks to this genetic wiring . . . I'll say, 'You betcha, I'll take a risk; I'll go walk out on a tightrope; I'll walk too far out into the ocean because I'm excited to see what it feels like.' It's just the way I am."

After receiving an undergraduate degree in speech pathology and audiology and a master's in communication disorders, Melinda soon put her newly certified skills to use as a school speech pathologist, only to find that this was not her life's calling. "I have always been at my best when spinning many plates in the air. To be a great speech pathologist, you must have the ability to be very focused on the minutest element of change over a very long and slow process. You must be incredibly patient. You spend most of your time isolated in a one-on-one situation [therapy]. I love to excel under a million deadlines, inspire teams to produce great results and try out new ideas. The two skill sets did not line up."

In a true "life is short" moment, she decided to go to Nashville for the months of summer vacation that came with being an employee of a school system. She felt that a season in a new setting would help her consider her life's direction with more clarity.

During that summer, a college acquaintance convinced Melinda to extend her stay and work with him in Nashville. He and his business partner had begun representing a new recording artist—a teenage girl they believed had a bright future. The artist's name was Amy Grant.

So began her involvement in the music industry of Nashville, a love relationship she has maintained throughout her professional career in one way or another. She spent a decade as a founding executive of Reunion Records before leaving to create a music distribution division for AOL/Time Warner's WEA Corp. As vice president and general manager, she developed and built the Warner Christian Division from the ground up. She followed that experience with four years of providing business management for top country music celebrities. Most recently Melinda has rejoined her husband, David, as a partner in their twelve-year-old brand management practice "to create innovative marketing strategies for companies with great products."

Of her unusual career journey, Melinda gets a bit philosophical: "For me, getting to where I am has been a series of shadings—a series of new doors that open and choices between a window or a door, and the one you go through leads you to the next place and you can't say that it was one particular door or window for me."

But for all the professional acclaim, nothing prepared her for becoming a mom in what she laughingly referred to as a "last gasp" attempt at motherhood. "I had the most amazing eureka moment because I had not really understood how amazing it is to be a woman," she happily remembered of her son's birth seven years ago. "When I had Alexander, I had this immediate connection, this euphoric feeling of being connected from generation to generation to generation— finally understanding the mystery of how women bring life into the world and how amazingly powerful that is."

While the wonder of the entire birthing process made an indelible imprint on her and left her forever changed, she's quick to explain that in the business world, "I don't wear my femininity on my sleeve. It's part of who I am, but . . . I don't remind people that I'm a woman when I make a presentation . . . I love being a woman, but it's not a characteristic that I feel defines me. It's part of the fabric of the tapestry of who I am."

For Gen Y young women just beginning their journey toward significance, Melinda counseled, "Believe in yourself— it's about totally recognizing the value that you have that is unique. You have what no one else in the entire universe ever has had or ever will have. A special combination of every-thing—it's an aggregate of physical, emotional, spiritual perspective; your height, your weight—everything about you is unique to the moment. And so, if you don't believe in yourself and you hold back, you're depriving the world of something that's so special that they will never have again."

As if to "walk the talk," Melinda confidently conveyed that she believes in herself and her abilities. When asked about the future of her business she said, "Success is not the end or a destination but is the process. We don't measure success by the number of bodies you employ or the revenue stream you generate. We've already been successful as many people measure it. We've had some amazing career moments. Success for us now lies in the times we are able to share our experience with our clients and see them grow and prosper. What is most important to me at this point in life is beyond career success. That being said, I am more than thrilled with this new path I'm on with David, and I have this strong belief that I have things left to do—important things, unique to my journey. So I'll take my own advice, take a risk, and step into unknown territory if necessary."

When asked what those important things might be, Melinda smiled and said, "Wait and see."

CHAPTER 11

Your Life Equity

Y ou've read about the power of a woman's life equity. You've read the stories of women who have used *their* equity to build the life they envisioned.

Now it is your turn. There are still chapters to write in the story of *you*! Use the space below to narrate your life's journey, identifying the qualities and skills you've acquired along the way.

_____

_____

_____

_____

_____

_____

History's Mentors

The annals of history brim with the stories of outstanding women who answered the call to leadership when it sounded. These women took the skills and experiences their journeys of life provided and applied them to higher things. We could call them "trailblazers of transference"!

Below are just a few whose examples have inspired and strengthened me on my journey.

Deborah—A Mother for Israel

If you are not familiar with the Old Testament, you may not have heard of an extraordinary woman named Deborah. She doesn't get as much press as her colleague and contemporary, Samson, but her exploits were just as amazing.

Roughly twelve centuries before the birth of Christ, Deborah was called upon to fill a leadership vacuum at a time when her people were divided, disorganized, and under attack. This was before the twelve tribes of Israel had united under a single king, for example, David or Solomon.

The biblical book of Judges tells us Deborah was a prophetess and judge (today she would be called a mediator), who dispensed her wisdom each day while sitting under a palm tree. The spot came to be known as "Deborah's Tree."

Members of the various Israelite tribes would come to her to settle their disputes. (Note: Conflict resolution is a key skill at which many women excel and that most organizations desperately need.)

In Deborah's day these fragmented, often squabbling tribes were coming under increasing attack by Philistine armies. This military pressure, combined with their own disunity, was threatening their very existence.

According to the biblical account, Deborah called one of the leading men of the tribes to the tree and gave him a word of instruction from the Lord. She told him that he was to assemble ten thousand men and prepare to take the fight to the Philistine armies.

This prominent gentleman would agree to God's directive on one condition. He would assemble this army only if Deborah agreed to go with them, leading the way into battle!

Now, it would have been easy and natural for Deborah to say, "Hey, I'm a judge, not a soldier. I deliver the word of the Lord. I've done my part. Now you go do yours." But that was not her response. She was a woman of faith, and she knew her country needed her. Though she had never gone into battle, she agreed to go—a prototypical Joan of Arc. But before she went she delivered one more prophetic prediction. The Bible records her words: "I will go with you. But because of the way you are going about this, the honor will not be yours, for the LORD will hand Sisera over to a woman."[1] Or to paraphrase: "Okay, but you need to know that I'm going to get the glory for this victory. Everyone's going to say that the big, bad Philistines were beaten by a girl!" And that is precisely what happened.

What has always impressed me is that in the critical moment, Deborah came to the aid of her country. I suspect she looked into the eyes of those Israelite leaders and saw men who were at a loss as to what to do. They were looking for a leader. Someone with confidence. Someone to pull them together as a unified, cohesive force.

Deborah became the mother of a nation that day. I can visualize her nurturing and encouraging them—scooping them up as we moms scoop up a hurting child. With boldness and courage she led them to a place of greater strength and security.

Israel went on to win a major victory. Deborah saved her nation, and an entire generation of Israelites experienced peace. And just as she had predicted, the military glory that might have gone to a man went to her instead. The book of Judges records for all generations "The Song of Deborah" composed to celebrate the victory she helped bring about. Here is just a portion of that beautiful tribute:

Listen, you kings!
Pay attention, you mighty rulers!
For I will sing to the LORD.
I will lift up my song to the LORD, the God of Israel.
LORD, when you set out from Seir
and marched across the fields of Edom,
the earth trembled and the cloudy skies poured down
rain.

The mountains quaked at the coming of the LORD.
Even Mount Sinai shook in the presence of the LORD,
the God of Israel.
In the days of Shamgar son of Anath,
and in the days of Jael,
people avoided the main roads,
and travelers stayed on crooked side paths.
There were few people left in the villages of Israel—
until Deborah arose as a mother for Israel.[2]

"Until Deborah arose . . ." What encouragement and resolve I have drawn from Deborah's example during the hard and scary places in my life.

Isabella of Castile—Visionary Queen

There are moments in time that radically alter the course of history. One such moment occurred when a woman stepped out and asserted herself when her husband was about to miss a historic opportunity.

Christopher Columbus was looking for a sponsor for an exploratory expedition to reach the Indies by sailing into the uncharted West. King Ferdinand of Spain tended to think the idea was crazy. But his queen, Isabella, stepped in and persuaded her husband to give the fellow a chance. As you know, the journey was successful, and the rest of the amazing story is still being written.

Though far from perfect and very much a product of her age, Isabella of Castile serves to remind us how important it can be for women to step across boundaries and explore new roles.

Sojourner Truth—Courage Personified

What tremendous inspiration I've found in the example of another Isabella who blazed new trails. The woman known to history as Sojourner Truth was born into slavery as Isabella Baumfree in Ulster County, New York, around the year 1797. Like breeding livestock, she was forced to bear five children with a man chosen by her owner. In 1827, around the age of thirty, she escaped to Canada taking her youngest child, Sophie, with her.

Sojourner returned to New York two years later when that state became one of the first to abolish slavery.

In time she became the first freed slave to sue for the release of her son and was a powerful and tireless advocate for the nationwide abolition of slavery as well as equal rights for women. One incident in particular from her long and fruitful life serves to illustrate the depth of her courage and the power of her conviction.

In 1851, a full ten years before the onset of the Civil War, Sojourner was invited to attend a Women's Convention in Akron, Ohio. Many of the people in attendance were either offended or alarmed by the presence of this outspoken black woman. Many begged Frances Gage, the meeting's organizer, to not allow her to speak.

On the second day of the conference, a number of ministers had been invited to participate in a discussion of the group's resolutions concerning women's rights. Here's what Frances Gage recorded about that day's events:

> Methodist, Baptist, Episcopal, Presbyterian, and Universalist ministers came in to hear and discuss the resolutions presented.

One claimed superior rights and privileges for men, on the ground of "superior intellect"; another, because of the "manhood of Christ; if God had desired the equality of woman, He would have given some token of His will through the birth, life, and death of the Saviour." Another gave us a theological view of the "sin of our first mother."

There were very few women in those days who dared to "speak in meeting," and the august teachers of the people were seemingly getting the better of us, while the boys in the galleries, and the sneerers among the pews, were hugely enjoying the discomfiture as they supposed, of the "strong-minded."

Some of the tender-skinned friends were on the point of losing dignity, and the atmosphere betokened a storm. When, slowly from her seat in the corner rose Sojourner Truth, who, till now, had scarcely lifted her head.

"Don't let her speak!" gasped half a dozen in my ear.

She moved slowly and solemnly to the front, laid her old bonnet at her feet, and turned her great speaking eyes to me. There was a hissing sound of disapprobation above and below.

I rose and announced, "Sojourner Truth," and begged the audience to keep silence for a few moments.

The tumult subsided at once, and every eye was fixed on this almost Amazon form, which stood nearly six feet high, head erect, and eyes piercing the upper air like one in a dream. At her first word there was a profound hush. She spoke in deep tones, which, though not loud, reached every ear in the house, and away through the throng at the doors and windows.[3]

Sojourner didn't speak long, and what she said was delivered in the crude, broken English of a former slave. But her words shook the building and reverberated through the whole country. One section in particular still rings like a liberty bell:

> Then that little man in black there, he says women can't have as much rights as men, 'cause Christ wasn't a woman. Where did your Christ come from, sir? Where did your Christ come from? From God and a woman! Man had nothing to do with Him.
>
> If the first woman God ever made was strong enough to turn the world upside down all alone, these women together ought to be able to turn it back, and get it right side up again! And now they are asking to do it.[4]

One hundred years before Rosa Parks took her courageous stand, Sojourner Truth was blazing trails to freedom.

Margaret Thatcher—The Iron Lady

Great Britain's first and only woman to hold the office of prime minister has always been a real hero to me. Margaret Thatcher rose to a leadership challenge at a moment in which the United Kingdom was in steep economic decline and a crisis of cultural confidence.

With determination, creativity, and consensus building, she effected changes no one dreamed possible. She turned her nation around and put it on the road to economic prosperity. Along the way, she showed the fortitude to fight for her country's interests. She guided Britain victoriously through the Falklands War and stood shoulder to shoulder with Ronald Reagan in facing down the global threat of the Soviet Union.

I believe Baroness Thatcher brilliantly exemplified the leadership qualities a woman can bring to a challenging situation. You can hear those qualities and values in the words she spoke on May 4, 1979, the history-making day she assumed the highest office in the land. As she stood on the threshold of 10 Downing Street, just before walking through that famous black door for the first time as prime minister, she said:

> I know full well the responsibilities that await me as I enter the door of No. 10 and I'll strive unceasingly to try to fulfill the trust and confidence that the British people have placed in me and the things in which I believe.
>
> And I would just like to remember some words of St. Francis of Assisi, which I think are really just particularly apt at the moment. "Where there is discord, may we bring harmony. Where there is error, may we bring truth. Where there is doubt, may we bring faith. And where there is despair, may we bring hope."
>
> And to all the British people—howsoever they voted—may I say this. Now that the Election is over, may we get together and strive to serve and strengthen the country of which we're so proud to be a part.
>
> And finally, one last thing: in the words of Airey Neave, "There is now work to be done."[5]

Indeed. And the same is true for you and me. In fact, it's the message of this book: "Our country needs us. We have work to do."

Notes

Chapter 1

1. John Maxwell, "Leadership Is Influence: Nothing More, Nothing Less," http://www.christianitytoday.com/bcl/areas/leadership/articles/090905.html.

2. Bob Boylan, *Get Everyone in Your Boat Rowing in the Same Direction: 5 Leadership Principles to Follow So Others Will Follow You* (Cincinnati: Adams Media Corporation, 1993), 13.

3. Patricia Aburdene and John Naisbitt, *Megatrends for Women* (New York: Ballantine Books, 1993).

Chapter 2

1. Roger H. Nye, *The Challenge of Command,* West Point Military History Series (San Marcos, CA: Perigee Trade, 2001).

2. Christopher Kolenda, *Leadership: The Warrior's Art,* 2nd ed. (Carlisle, PA: Army War College Foundation Press, July 2001).

3. Owen Connelly, *On War and Leadership: The Words of Combat Commanders from Frederick the Great to Norman Schwarzkopf* (Princeton, NJ: Princeton University Press, August 2002).

4. W. J. Wood, *Leaders and Battles: The Art of Military Leadership* (New York: Presidio Press, 1995).

5. Eliot A. Cohen, *Supreme Command: Soldiers, Statesmen, and Leadership in Wartime* (New York: Free Press, June 2002).

6. Wess Roberts, *The Leadership Secrets of Attila the Hun*, New Ed ed. (New York: Bantam Doubleday Dell, 1990).

7. United Kingdom Franchise Survey, "Failure fears deter women from enterprise," http://www.startups.co.uk/Failure_fears_deter_women_from_enterprise .html

8. Ibid.

9. Cheryl Dahle, "Natural Leader," *Fast Company*, November 2000, 268.

10. Brian Wu and Anne Marie Knott, "Entrepreneurial Risk and Market Entry," *Management Science* 52, no. 9 (2006): 1315–1330.

11. Ibid.

12. Nancy Ammon Jianakoplos and Alexandra Bernasek, "Are women more risk averse? (attitude toward financial risk)," *Economic Inquiry* (1998), http://www.accessmylibrary.com/comsite5/bin/pdinventory.pl?pdlanding=1&referid=2930&purchase_type=ITM&item_id=0286-5597449.

13. Kristi Hedges, "Women Entrepreneurs and Risk," *Entrepreneur Magazine*, January 17, 2007, http://www.entrepreneur.com/management/leadership/article173126.html.

14. Ericka N. Dennis, "The Influence of Risk-Taking Personality on Behavior in Romantic Relationships"(paper, McKendree University, Lebanon, IL) http://faculty.mckendree.edu/scholars/winter2005/dennis.htm.

15. Johann Wolfgang von Goethe, quoted in Ted Goodman, ed., *The Forbes Book of Business Quotations* (New York: Black Dog & Leventhal Publishers, 1997), 96.

16. Albert L. Winseman, Donald O. Clifton, and Curt Liesveld, *Living*

Your Strengths: Discover Your God-given Talents and Inspire Your Community (New York: Gallup Press, 2003), 3.

17. Tom Rath, *StrengthsFinder 2.0* (New York: Gallup Press, 2007), 7, 8.

18. Lynn Matlock Hicks, "10 Secrets for Women Leaders to Increase Visibility and Credibility," *divine.ca*, 2008, www.divine.ca/en/ career-and-money/articles/c_20_i_1/10-secrets-for-women-leaders-l.html.

19. Anna Fels, "Do Women Lack Ambition," *Harvard Business Review* (March 2005)

Chapter 3

1. Glenn Van Ekeren, ed., *Speaker's Sourcebook II:Quotes, Stories, & Anecdotes for Every Occasion* (Englewood Cliffs, NJ: Prentice Hall, 1994), 76.

2. Rutherford Birchard Hayes, *Diary and Letters of Rutherford Birchard Hayes: Nineteenth President of the United States,* vol. II, Charles Richard Williams, ed. The Ohio State Archaeological and Historical Society, 5 vols. (1922–1926), Diary (December 16, 1861), 160.

3. Timothy Ferriss, *The 4-Hour Workweek* (New York: Crown Publishers, 2007), 46.

4. George Eliot [Mary Ann Evans], *Felix Holt, the Radical,* (City: Publisher, date of edition),

5. Ferriss, 46.

6. Brian Tracy, "A Special Kind of Courage," Brian Tracy International http://blogs.briantracy.com/public/blog/167740.

7. *Speaker's Sourcebook II,* 329.

8. Pat Lynch, "Flex Your Muscle," *Women's Radio News,* June 2007, http://www.womensradio.com/content/templates/?a=15&z=0.

9. Bo Bennett, "Inspiration from Debbi Fields Rose," *Year to Success Online*, 2007, http://www.yeartosuccess.com/public/Inspiration_ from_Debbi_Fields_Rose.html.

10. Thomas J. Peters and Robert H. Waterman, *In Search of Excellence: Lessons from America's Best-Run Companies* (New York: HarperCollins Publishers, 1982).

11. Henrietta Mears, quoted in George Sweeting, ed., *Who Said That?* (Chicago: Moody Press, 1994), 20.

12. Ferriss, 47.

13. Vincent O'Sullivan, ed., *The Collected Letters of Katherine Mansfield*, vol. 2 (New York: Oxford University Press, 1996), 125.

Chapter 4

1. Numerous scientific studies have shown a link between testosterone levels and behavioral factors such as risk tolerance, assertiveness, and competitive intensity. Of course, this is just one of many factors that influence our behaviors and attitudes. Hormones alone are not destiny.

2. William L. Cron of Texas Christian University in Fort Worth, John L. Graham and Mary C. Gilly of the University of California at Irvine, and John W. Slocum Jr. "A Behavioral Study of Pricing Decisions: A Focus on Gender," Southern Methodist University, Dallas, TX.

3. Brian Amble, "Why Do Women in Business Sell Themselves Short?" *Management-Issues*, 17, August 2006, http://www. management-issues.com/2006/8/20/research/why-do-women-in-business-sell-themselves-short.asp.

4. Jane Herman, "Beyond Compare," *Success Tools with Jane Herman*, Women in Technology International, http://www.witi.com/ growth/2005/compare.php.

5. Peggy Klaus, *Brag! The Art of Tooting Your Own Horn Without Blowing It* (New York: Warner Books, 2003), 6.

6. T. Roberts, "Gender and the influences of evaluation on self-assessment in achievement settings," *Psychological Bulletin* (1991), 297–308.

7. Sheila Brownlow, Rebecca Whitener, and Janet M. Rupert, " 'I'll take gender differences for $1000!' domain-specific intellectual success on *Jeopardy*," *Sex Roles: A Journal of Research* (1998), http://findarticles.com/p/articles/mi_m2294/is_n3-4_v38/ai_20574388/pg_1.

8. Mark 9:35.

9. Klaus, 17.

Chapter 5

1. *Body dysmorphic disorder*—pathological preoccupation with an imagined or slight physical defect of one's body to the point of causing significant stress or behavioral impairment in several areas (as work and personal relationships). *Merriam-Webster's Medical Dictionary* (Springfield, MA: Merriam-Webster, Inc., 2002).

2. http://www.rocketquiz.com.

3. http://web.tickle.com/.

4. Gary Smalley, "Discovering the Value of Your Personality," Smalley Relationship Center, http://www.smalleyonline.com/articles/i_discoveringpersonality.html.

5. http://www.thecolorcode.com.

6. As of the time of publication, these and similar tests are available at a modest cost from numerous online sources including: www.careerkey.com and www.self-directed-search.com.

7. "Madam C. J. Walker—a brief bio of the famous entrepreneur, philanthropist, and political activist," Madam C. J. Walker: the

Official Web site, http://www.madamecjwalker.com/bio_madam_
cj_walker.html.

Chapter 6

1. Seneca, *On a Happy Life, 2 (L'Estrange's Abstract, Chapter i)*.
2. Tom Morris, *True Success: A New Philosophy of Excellence* (New
   York: Berkley Books, 1994), 183.
3. Ibid., 48.
4. Gregg Levoy, *Callings: Finding and Following and Authentic Life*
   (New York: Three Rivers Press, 1997), 69.
5. This quote is attributed to various individuals, including Napoleon
   Hill, Norman Vincent Peale, and Muhammad Ali.

Chapter 7

1. Anne Marie Chaker, "Business Schools Target Stay-at-Home
   Moms," *Wall Street Journal*, May 10, 2006.
2. Ann Crittenden, "Leadership Begins at Home," *eNotAlone.com*,
   http://www.enotalone.com/article/6340.html.
3. Ibid, http://www.enotalone.com/article/6340.html.
4. Ibid.
5. Catharine E. Beecher, *A Treatise on Domestic Economy, for the Use of
   Young Ladies at Home and at School* (Boston: Thomas H. Webb &
   Company, 1843), 156.
6. Ann Crittenden, "Multitasking and the Rise of the Life Manager,"
   eNotAlone.com. http://www.enotalone.com/article/6343.html.
7. Joann S. Lublin, "Why Women Must Hone Their Negotiating
   Skills," CareerJournal.com, *Wall Street Journal*, http://www.
   careerjournal.com/columnists/manageyourcareer/20031105-
   managingyourcareer.html?home_whatsnew_minor.
8. Op. Cit. Crittenden, "Why women Must Hone Their Negotiating

Skills".

9. "Margaret Brown," www.wikipedia.org. http://en.wikipedia.org/
wiki/Molly_Brown (9 September 2007).

10. Ann Crittenden, "Efficiency," eNotAlone.com, http://www.
enotalone.com/article/6345.html.

Life Equity Profile #7

1. http://www.wpafb.af.mil/library/factsheets/factsheet.
asp?id=6234.

Chapter 8

1. Doc Childre and Bruce Cryer, *From Chaos to Coherence* (Boulder
Cree, CA: Heartmath, 2000).

2. "Women in the Labor Force: A Databook," Dept. of Labor, Bureau
of Labor Statistics, May 2005.

3. "Fact Sheet: July 2007," National Business Women's Council, www.
nwbc.gov. http://www.nwbc.gov/ResearchPublications/docu-
ments/KeyFactsWBOandtheirEnterprises.pdf.

4. Ibid.

5. Joanna L. Krotz, "Do Women Make Better Managers?" *Microsoft
Small Business Center*, Microsoft. http://www.microsoft.com/
smallbusiness/resources/management/leadership_training/do_
women_make_better_managers.mspx?xid=OVPI181#bio1.

6. Wally Bock, "They May Be Soft Skills, But They're Real Important,"
Three Star Leadership, http://www.threestarleadership.com/
articles/soft_skills.htm.

7. http://accepted.typepad.com/admissions_almanac.

8. Linda Abraham, "Leadership Starts with Trust," *Accepted
Admissions Almanac*, Accepted.com. http://accepted.typepad.com/
admissions_almanac/2005/04/garnering_trust.html.

9. Ibid.

10. Ibid.

11. Bob Boylan, 13.

12. Ibid., 14.

13. George Matthew Adams, *The Forbes Book of Business Quotations: 14,266 Thoughts on the Business of Life* (New York: Black Dog & Leventhal Publishers, 1997).

14. Bessie Stanley, published 11/30/1905 in the Lincoln (Kansas) *Sentinel.* An adaptation of this is often attributed to Ralph Waldo Emerson, though nothing like it has been found in his writings.

Chapter 9

1. Pamela McLean, "The Art of Leading from Behind in Our Coaching," The Hudson Institute, http://www.hudsoninstitute. com/images/PDF/WP_LeadingBehind.pdf.

2. John Maxwell, *The 21 Irrefutable Laws of Leadership: Follow Them and People Will Follow You,* (Nashville, TN: Thomas Nelson, 1998), 139, 140.

3. Donna Brooks and Lynn Brooks, *Seven Secrets of Successful Women: Strategies of the Women Who've Made It* (New York: MJF Books, 1997), 19.

4. Ibid., 21.

5. Glenn Van Ekeren, ed., *Speaker's Sourcebook II* (Englewood Cliffs, NJ: Prentice Hall, 1994), 329.

6. Ibid., 374.

Chapter 10

1. "James Truslow Adams," ThinkExist.com. http://thinkexist.com/ quotes/james_truslow_adams/.

2. Vickie L. Milazzo, *Inside Every Woman: Using the 10 Strengths You Didn't Know You Had to Get the Career and Life You Want Now*

(Hoboken, NJ: John Wiley & Sons, 2006), 5.

3. Michelle Nunn, *Be the Change!: Change the World. Change Yourself* (Atlanta: Hundreds of Heads Books, 2006), x–xi.

Appendix A

1. Judges 4:9 (NIV).
2. Judges 5:3–7 (NLT).
3. *History of Woman Suffrage*, 2nd ed. vol.1 (Rochester, NY: Charles Mann, 1889), edited by Elizabeth Cady Stanton, Susan B. Anthony, and Matilda Joslyn Gage.
4. "Ain't I a Woman?" speech by Sojourner Truth, Wikisource, http://en.wikisource.org/wiki/Ain%27t_I_a_Woman%3F.
5. http://www.margaretthatcher.org/speeches/displaydocument.asp?docid=104078

Acknowledgments

I appreciate the help of many for their work and encouragement during the writing of this book, but most of all I would like to thank my parents, Hilman and Mary Jo Wedgeworth. They modeled the truth that "leadership is not as it appears, but as it performs" by showing us each day that actions speak louder than words. Thank you, Mom and Dad, for the lessons that are well taught. I hope they were well learned and that I have done an adequate job of passing them along.

The family of a writer ends up serving as the sounding board for thoughts and snippets as they are transformed into sentences and paragraphs. My husband, Chuck Blackburn, has encouraged with insight and humor—and I thank him. Our daughter, Mary Morgan Ketchel, and her husband, Paul, have provided helpful opinions and our son, Chad, has maintained a patient interest in his excited mother's progress reports.

Tea Hickman Hoffman has been a friend in providing advice to a rookie writer. Esther Fedorkevich served as my agent for this project, steering us along the right paths and believing that there is equity and value in every woman's life. My deep gratitude to both.

During over twenty years of giving speeches and speaking in seminars, I have talked to thousands of women about leadership and my hopes that they will step forward and use their gifts to create a better life in their corners of the world. I want to thank the many women from these audiences who have shared their successes and failures with me. They have assured me that women do indeed want the opportunity to make a difference in our world, and it is these same women who have encouraged me to expand my thoughts into this book.

I have grown to appreciate just how much work and effort is required to consolidate years of speeches, written columns and recorded comments into a volume that will hopefully be enjoyed by many, and inspirational to women who are seeking to add value and texture to their lives. For their guidance and leadership in navigating this lengthy process, I would like to thank Chartwell Literary Group (www.chartwellliterary.com).

Finally, I feel special gratitude for the friendship and wisdom of the women in my life whose rich stories have inspired this book. Thank you for sharing your lives with me.

About the Author

Marsha Blackburn is a wife, mother, and business woman. A skilled and competent legislator, she solves problems and is a respected leader.

Marsha was born in Laurel, Mississippi where she excelled in 4H club, was an interested student and an accomplished musician. She graduated from Mississippi State University in 1973 where she spent her summers selling books door to door for the Southwestern Company. She was a student manager and a sales manager, playing a major role in the company's establishment of a women's division. Later as a small business owner, she was actively involved in Tennessee grassroots politics. She served as the Executive Director of the Tennessee Film, Entertainment, and Music Commission, was elected to the state senate, and, in 2002 was elected to serve in the U.S. House of Representatives. (In the tradition of earlier Tennessee women who served in the House, Marsha prefers the title *Congressman.*)

In Congress, Marsha has held leadership posts with the

Republican Study Committee and the National Republican Congressional Committee. She holds a seat on the prestigious Energy and Commerce Committee, is a Deputy Whip, and co-chair of the Congressional Songwriters Caucus. She has co-chaired the Congressional Art competition, been appointed to the Joint Committee on Taxation, and the Select Committee on Energy, Environment and Global Warming. In 2003, she was successful in securing sales tax deductability from federal income tax filing for all states without a state income tax.

Named a "Rising Star" by the Capitol Hill newspaper, *Roll Call*, and the "Best New Member" by *Washingtonian* magazine, Blackburn has developed a reputation for being a person of high energy and action. She is annually recognized by pro-business, pro-family, pro-life, and anti-tax groups for her voting record. In 2007, the Recording Academy honored her with the Congressional Grammy for her exceptional work on intellectual property and entertainment issues.

In 2006, Marsha's sorority, Chi Omega, named her their national Woman of Achievement. In 2007, she was named a distinguished alumni for Mississippi State University.

She and Chuck Blackburn have been married for over 30 years and have 2 adult children and 1 grandchild.